BAS
BUT
BRILLIANT

Genevieve McGough.

Brilliant food made easy.

Written & photographed by Genevieve McGough.

PENGUIN BOOKS
Published by the Penguin Group
Penguin Group (NZ), cnr Airborne and Rosedale Roads, Albany,
Auckland 1310, New Zealand (a division of Pearson New Zealand Ltd)
Penguin Group (USA) Inc., 375 Hudson Street,
New York, New York 10014, USA
Penguin Group (Canada), 90 Eglinton Avenue East, Suite 7000, Toronto,
Ontario, M4P 2Y3, Canada (a division of Pearson Penguin Canada Inc.)
Penguin Books Ltd, 80 Strand, London, WC2R 0RL, England
Penguin Ireland, 25 St Stephen's Green,
Dublin 2, Ireland (a division of Penguin Books Ltd)
Penguin Group (Australia), 250 Camberwell Road, Camberwell,
Victoria 3124, Australia (a division of Pearson Australia Group Pty Ltd)
Penguin Books India Pvt Ltd, 11, Community Centre,
Panchsheel Park, New Delhi - 110 017, India
Penguin Books (South Africa) (Pty) Ltd, 24 Sturdee Avenue,
Rosebank, Johannesburg 2196, South Africa

Penguin Books Ltd, Registered Offices: 80 Strand, London, WC2R 0RL, England

First published by Penguin Group (NZ), 2005
1 3 5 7 9 10 8 6 4 2

Designed and typeset by seven.co.nz
Prepress by microdot
Printed by Condor Production, Hong Kong

ISBN 0 14 301991 0

A catalogue record for this book is available from the National Library of New Zealand.

www.penguin.co.nz

BASIC BUT BRILLIANT

Genevieve McGough.

For my parents for teaching me about food, wine and cooking from as far back as I can remember.

A special thank you to: My partner Charles for investing in a computer so I could start writing. Dilowar Hussein at Quickweb for creating my wonderful website - www.genevievescuisine.com. Anja Gallas for her photographic advice. Mantells for allowing me take produce photographs. Sara Bellamy at seven for her patience and for raising my photographic standards. My agent Glenys Bean for taking me on and giving me endless media advice. And Bernice Beachman and Philippa Gerrard at Penguin Books for the fantastic opportunity to write this book.

Penguin Group

07 **Introduction.**

01

15 **Classic Dressings.**

16 Hollandaise
24 Cream sauce
32 Mayonnaise and aïoli
42 Vinaigrette
52 Pesto and pistou

04

91 **Vegetarian.**

92 Polenta
100 Risotto
108 Creamy mashed potato
116 Batters and fritters

05

07

183 **Shopping Guide.**

187 **Index.**

64 Hot smoking fish and vegetables
72 Slow-cooked meats
83 Brining meats

02

03

63 **Fish & Meat.**

128 Meringue pies
138 Jelly
144 Parfait
150 Poached fruit and fruit syrups
156 Crème brûlée and custard pots
163 The beauty of pavlova
170 Cheesecake

127 **Sweets.**

06

179 **Glossary.**

08

Introduction.

01

While there are many cookbooks available on the market, few concentrate on teaching actual cooking methods. Instead, they largely consist of a collection of recipes that home cooks can copy and then attempt to present like the photographs in the book. I feel it is important therefore to teach people more about the basics of cooking in order to help them understand how a chef designs a dish.

Part of what a chef knows is how to incorporate different flavours into a recipe as well as which flavours will work. If I can teach you that knowledge, then you have the freedom to experiment with flavours and work them into a chosen dish. In short, I have written a book that I know would have been extremely useful for me before I started cooking in a professional kitchen.

I like flavour combinations to be complete, uncomplicated yet inspiring, and made with readily available ingredients. While I give many options for flavouring a recipe, I always suggest how many flavours to keep to, avoiding flavour confusion. My basic rule with flavour combinations is the apple never falls far from the tree. I use very few fusion combinations and limit the flavourings to one ethnic background. I think this is especially important for inexperienced cooks. Not many complicated combinations of flavours, for example in desserts, are preferable to a good old-fashioned serving of chocolate mousse and softly whipped cream. In my opinion, there is no need to try hard—just concentrate on obtaining great tasting food through traditional methods.

Why do seemingly unusual food combinations work so well together? To understand the way food flavours affect our taste-buds, we need to first understand how the human tongue tastes different types of flavours.

The most negative aspect of the tongue is the taste-buds at the back and rear sides. Imagine putting soap in your mouth! Is your tongue curling at the thought in horror? Notice it is at the back of your tongue you imagine this. While that flavour is negative, slight bitterness can also be a positive flavour in a combination, so pleasant flavours are tasted at the back of the tongue as well.

The tongue senses sweetness and saltiness on the tip. Sourness and some saltiness are sensed from along the sides and centre front of the tongue. When a chef tastes a sauce to see if enough salt has been added, he concentrates on the roll-over-the-tongue feeling enough salt gives the tongue. The pleasurable taste sensation of enough salt moves from one edge of the tongue to the other and over the tip. Too much salt and, you've guessed it, tongue curl! Only a little of what we taste comes from the centre of the tongue as the taste-buds are largely located around the edge.

My most vivid memories of childhood revolve around food.

One of the most common taste combinations is sweet and sour. I believe the reason we enjoy this flavour combination so much is that more than one set of our positive taste-buds are stimulated. Some of the more obvious ways to use the sweet and sour combination is in pickling brines, relishes, Chinese food sauces such as sweet and sour pork, and to a lesser extent salad dressings. Vinegar is usually accompanied with sugar and salt when used in a recipe, and if you think about the areas of your taste-buds being stimulated (all of them), you can understand why this combination is so pleasant. The tastiest meals incorporate all these factors into the finished dish.

Home cooks become used to seeing a pinch of salt in the list of ingredients, or a vague instruction such as 'season with salt'. It is not clear how much to add. All my recipes have the salt measured via measuring spoons. While meat needs only a sprinkle of salt, recipes such as sauces and stews require a reasonable amount to bring out the appropriate flavours. Even the best recipe can seem bland if there isn't enough seasoning. Never heap the measuring spoon with salt: flatten off the mound to avoid over-seasoning, and avoid measuring with cutlery as spoons vary in size from brand to brand.

For the trickier recipes in this book, I have included as many tips as possible to avert disaster and wasted ingredients. While this means some reading is involved before making the recipes, it is better to know up front what can go wrong rather than trying to fix it afterwards. In addition, I like all the ingredients to be used up with nothing left over. For example, poaching liquor is reduced down for a sauce and never wasted. While leftovers might be nice the next day, throwing away extra recipe ingredients is annoying and wasteful. I avoid this at all times.

Most home cooks have a basic range of equipment. I love ice-cream, but who has an ice-cream churning machine? I have devised recipes that do not require equipment most of us don't own. On the odd occasion, I might suggest a specific piece of equipment, but I never assume the reader has an ice-cream churning machine or a deep fryer, for example. My goal is for the reader to make tasty food, with readily available ingredients and as little fuss as possible.

Lastly, I have included recipes that are old favourites, as well as innovative new recipes with variations, so the reader can build a solid, quality recipe collection that caters to many different tastes. While this book will be a useful reference, I'd also like to broaden your mind with other possibilities.

My history.

Oddly, my most vivid memories of childhood revolve around food. My father used to take me to the old Bonanza supermarket where the friendly staff in the delicatessen would let me sample all the exotic meats and pickles. I was drawn to food at an early age, and the passion has stayed with me during my career. I expect it will remain with me for my lifetime.

While still very young, I would strive to make coconut ice and fudge better than my older sister. By the time I got to cooking class in school I was pestering the teachers constantly for information they just didn't have. I was told to sit down and stop being so demanding, but oddly this did not happen to me in any other classes. My parents both worked, so I would cook dinner for them, and I loved to buy and read cookbooks whenever I had the opportunity.

I remember reading a children's book called *Little Richard*. In the story, the two characters made biscuits and those biscuits looked pretty damn good to me. However, I had no recipe, so I just made them up and they worked! I don't think they were all that nice to eat but they smelt great. I was about thirteen and hooked on cooking!

When I left school, I worked for two years in the best catering company in Auckland – Austins Catering. The food was upmarket and stunning so I was most fortunate to be employed there. In those days cooking schools did not accept you until you had completed 2000 hours in a professional kitchen, so I started out as a dishwasher and worked for eight months in a separate room, glimpsing the food as it went by. However, they knew I was keen and I was soon promoted to commis chef, helping at functions and carrying out basic prep work in the main kitchen. I was in heaven at this stage, as I had never seen or tasted food of this calibre before.

From there I worked around the upmarket Auckland restaurant scene with a stint in a small café, and later took a job at GPK restaurant. Under the guidance of owner Dominique Parat, I learnt to leave fusion cooking behind and move on to a classic French style of cuisine, which was like a breath of fresh air. I never went back to fusion cooking. My time with Dominique was so successful I opened his third GPK restaurant in Takapuna as head chef. Now, having trained my replacement, I have decided to pursue a career in food writing and photography to explore my creativity in recipes through teaching via books.

It is incredible how much I have learnt while writing this book. Chefs carry much information about cooking in their heads, but few have the chance to put that knowledge into writing in order to teach others. I hope I can inspire you to learn about and love cooking as much as I do.

Classic Dressings.

02

Hollandaise sauce originated from 19th century French cuisine, meaning Holland-style or from Holland. Most historians agree that it was originally called Sauce Isigny, after a town in Normandy known for its butter. During World War I, butter production came to a halt in France and butter was imported from Holland to supply the demand. The name of the sauce was changed to hollandaise, to indicate where the butter came from, and was never changed back.

Today, hollandaise is used in restaurants the world over as a decadent, savoury, citrus sauce. As lemon is the main flavouring, it is generally paired with seafood, freshwater fish and crustaceans. However, the sauce often features as an accompaniment to vegetable dishes – everything from vegetable medleys to plain steamed asparagus can be jazzed up to restaurant quality with the addition of hollandaise.

Let's not forget the most famous hollandaise dishes of all – Eggs Benedict and Eggs Florentine – which feature on almost every brunch menu around town. It is unclear exactly where the dishes developed, although the two most common references both claim patrons with the surname of Benedict requested a change of menu in American restaurants, so the chef, liking the dish, placed it on the menu. As an easy vegetarian option for restaurants, crispy bacon was swapped for spinach thus creating Eggs Florentine. These days other ingredients such as smoked salmon and avocado are commonly swapped for the bacon and all make a tasty and filling breakfast. Legend says it can cure a hangover, but the jury is still out on that one!

I have been wondering how to write an easy method for making hollandaise. Why, you ask? The problem is that, while easy to demonstrate, hollandaise couldn't be more difficult to explain in writing. However, when people ask me for a recipe, nine out of ten times it's for that delicious butter sauce. So, I have written down absolutely everything I can possibly think of to ensure ease of use for the keen at-home brunch chef.

Basic hollandaise recipe.

200g salted butter*
2 egg yolks
2 tablespoons lemon juice
1/2 teaspoon finely grated lemon zest
2 tablespoons white wine vinegar

*If you have unsalted butter, add ¼ teaspoon of salt to the sauce. You do not need to add any salt if the butter is salted but check the seasoning at the end anyway.

Prep.

Melt the butter 5 minutes or so ahead of time so that the milk solids sink to the bottom. This is important because when the butter is whisked in it allows better control of the consistency of the sauce.

Place a large pot filled to one-third with water on medium heat to boil. In a stainless-steel mixing bowl that sits on top of the pot but does not touch the water, place the egg yolks, lemon juice, lemon zest, and vinegar.

Turn the heat down to just under a simmer, the ideal heat that won't cook the yolks too fast. Sit the bowl over the water and gently whisk the yolk mixture. It will slowly start to heat and increase in volume.

Whisking is not to aerate the mixture so much as to avoid the yolks catching and to ensure even thickening. The yolk mixture will become a little thicker on the bottom and around the edges. Hold a towel around the outside of the bowl to remove it from the heat if it starts to form lumps from heating too fast.

Keep the yolk mixture moving by whisking continuously. The bubbles that form get smaller and smaller and soon become the larger part of the yolk mix as the runny yolk cooks. If it starts to catch, lift the bowl above the pot to slow down the heating. In about 5 to 10 minutes, the yolk mixture will hold its shape like softly whipped cream and the texture should be as smooth. This means the yolks are cooked but not to the point of being scrambled and you have made yourself what is called in French cooking a sabayon.

Sabayon can also be made with egg yolks and sugar. This is the base for many well-known recipes such as parfait and semi fredo (semi-frozen parfait with a fair amount of alcohol, for example tequila, added). The technique is also used as a base for decadent cakes.

Next, whisk in the butter. Make sure the butter is still hot. Place the sabayon bowl onto a damp cloth so it won't spin while you whisk. While whisking quickly, slowly pour in a steady but very thin stream of butter.

Don't add more butter than you can whisk in – if the sabayon is overloaded it will split the mixture (be patient, especially if you are a beginner). At first the whisking is quite easy, but as the butter is slowly incorporated it becomes a little tougher. Add the butter more slowly at this stage to compensate.

As you near the milk solids, do not add too much as the hollandaise is more likely to split at this stage. Slowly pour in the milk solids while still whisking, in order to loosen the hollandaise and set the consistency. Usually adding all the milk solids is the correct amount of moisture the hollandaise needs, but sometimes it can be too much so add slowly to check the consistency does not get too thin.

Alternatively, if you have added all the milk solids and it is still thicker than you would like, add a little boiling water. Variation can occur due to the size of the eggs. Check the seasoning, transfer to a small stainless-steel bowl and cover with cling film. Keep in a warm place until serving time. Hollandaise can safely be made up to 2 hours before needed.

If the butter has been added too fast and has split slightly, use a blender to blitz the emulsion and save it. Keep the sauce warm – if it cools too much the butter will start to set and, you guessed it, split, the dreaded term for all chefs.

Variations.

Lime hollandaise

Use lime zest and juice instead of lemon zest and juice in the basic recipe. Like lemon hollandaise, serve with any kind of seafood or freshwater fish and crustaceans.

Basil hollandaise

Add chopped basil to the finished hollandaise – perfect in spring with new season asparagus and a great sauce for vegetables. Other herbs also suit hollandaise: try sorrel, chervil, dill and parsley.

Béarnaise sauce

Swap the lemon juice for strong tarragon vinegar and omit the lemon zest. Add chopped fresh tarragon, chervil and parsley at the end and season well with freshly milled black pepper. If you don't have all those herbs, just use one, preferably tarragon. The best red meat sauce ever!

Works Benedict. p.19

Works Benedict.

Serves 4

120g fresh spinach
1/4 cup white vinegar
8 fresh organic eggs
4 English muffins
8 rashers bacon
1 avocado
1 quantity hollandaise (p.17)

Prep.

Place a litre of water in a medium-sized pot and bring to the boil.

Pick off all the spinach leaves, leaving as little stalk as possible.

Put some iced water in a mixing bowl. Quickly dip the spinach leaves into the simmering water, then put them straight into the iced water. Just wilt the leaves instead of blanching them so they don't lose too much of their leafy volume.

When cold, drain well and set aside. This can be done the night before.

To poach the eggs

Egg poaching! Easy you say? Done it thousands of times before? Here are some great tips. Make sure the eggs are as fresh as possible. If the cooked eggs are not completely white with the yolk in the centre, they could be old.

Place 2 litres water and ¼ cup white vinegar in a 4-litre pot and bring to the boil. Break the eggs into cups then turn down the heat to a slow simmer. Stir the water in a small whirlpool then tip the eggs into the simmering water. Poach about 6 to 8 eggs at a time and gently simmer for 3 minutes. Reheat the water each time more eggs are added if repeating the process. Drain eggs on paper towels and serve immediately.

To serve.

Cut the muffins in half and toast lightly under the grill until golden brown.

Meanwhile, fry the bacon strips in a pan until very crisp, then drain on paper towels.

Keep the bacon and muffins warm in the oven while assembling the other components.

Slice the avocados into 6 slices per avocado half.

Place 2 halves of muffin onto each plate and cover with wilted spinach leaves. Arrange the bacon on top of the spinach, then the avocado slices. Add an egg to each muffin half, then spoon hollandaise over the top. Serve immediately.

Caviar.

Wheaten blinis with smoked fish, caviar and hollandaise. p.23

Wheaten blinis with smoked fish, caviar and hollandaise.

Serves 4

10g dried yeast
½ teaspoon sugar
150ml milk
150ml warm water
200g plain flour
1 egg, separated
1 tablespoon butter, melted
½ teaspoon salt
vegetable oil for the pan
400g smoked tuna or other smoked fish
caviar
⅔ cup hollandaise (p.17)
olive oil for drizzling
freshly ground black pepper

Prep.

If you have blini pans then cook individual portions, otherwise cook an ordinary-sized pancake and slice it into quarters to serve.

Stir together the yeast, sugar, milk and warm water in a medium-sized mixing bowl. Set aside for 10 minutes to activate the yeast.

Sift in the flour and whisk until the batter is free of lumps. Whisk in the egg yolk, butter and salt.

In a separate bowl whisk the egg white until very fluffy and holds it shape when the beater passes through it. This is called the stiff peak stage. Using a metal spoon, fold the egg white into the batter.

Cover the batter and let it sit in a warm place for 30 minutes before cooking.

Set a medium-sized frying pan on the lowest heat possible and allow the pan to come to full temperature. The trick is to let the blinis cook as slowly as possible. Add about 1 tablespoon of cooking oil to the pan, then swirl the oil around to cover the base. Keep paper towels handy to wipe a little more oil on the pan surface between each blini to prevent sticking.

Pour 1 ladle of batter into the centre of the pan and let it settle on the base. When batter is bubbling on top and golden brown on the bottom, flip the blini and leave for another few minutes.

Remove from the pan and drain on a tray lined with paper towels. Keep warm in the oven while cooking the other blinis.

To serve.

Slice the blinis into 4 and arrange on 4 serving plates. Top with the smoked fish and caviar. Spoon on hollandaise to drip down one side (so people can see what they are eating). Drizzle with olive oil and sprinkle with freshly ground black pepper. Serve immediately.

Cream sauce.

How do chefs in fancy restaurants get all that flavour into a cream sauce? There are many tricks and variations, so I have narrowed down the options to the most common flavourings used to create tasty and creamy dishes. If you have guests, prepare the basic recipe ahead of time then reheat at serving time to cut down on the workload. Do not add the butter until just before serving.

If serving pasta, it can be cooked, cooled, tossed in a little cooking oil and reheated in the sauce at serving time.

If preparing cream sauce ahead of time, refrigerate when it has cooled to room temperature as cream can turn if left out in the heat for too long. Its shelf life is about 2–3 days for storage, so cover well with cling film or secure in an airtight container to keep fridge odours from tainting the delicate flavour.

White wine cream sauce is a versatile basic kitchen sauce that can be used for meat and fish sauces, pasta dishes and seafood entrées to name a few. Make the recipe in a pot as per the basic recipe and gently reduce the ingredients together or use the deglazing method as follows.

Deglazing.

The most common method of making white wine cream sauce in an à la carte restaurant is to deglaze the pan used to cook the meat for the dish with the wine. This way all the meat juices still in the pan incorporate with the wine for extra flavour. It sounds difficult but it is quite a simple method.

Chefs use a constantly hot oven and many ovenproof frying pans. The meat is seared in the pan with hot oil or clarified butter, then placed into the oven to finish cooking. When the meat is cooked and removed from the pan, any sauce base ingredients such as capers, onion or mushrooms are added and cooked gently for a couple of minutes. The pan is then flashed with wine or brandy to capture all the meat juices and any seasonings left in the pan, transferring the flavours to the sauce.

Next, the cream is added to the hot pan and reduced quickly on a gas element. The sauce is finished with a knob of butter for a glossy smooth finish. This technique is only suitable for cooking at home for 2 or 3 people. Larger numbers require the pot technique to cope with the quantity.

Straining.

It is completely up to the individual as to whether or not the sauce is strained through a fine mesh sieve after the reducing has finished. After deglazing a pan, cream sauce is usually strained to remove any traces of cooked meat and to leave a smooth glossy sauce. I rarely strain a white wine cream sauce as I like the onions and garlic left in for texture and flavour, but if the visual element is affected, as with red meat deglazing, then strain the sauce.

Basic white wine cream sauce recipe.

1 tablespoon butter
½ small white onion, finely chopped
2 small cloves garlic, peeled and minced
½ cup white wine
⅔ cup heavy cream
¼ teaspoon salt
1 knob butter

Prep.

In a large pot, add butter and sweat the onions and garlic, without colouring them, for 2 minutes. Pour on the wine, then reduce the liquid to two-thirds.

Add the cream and salt. Reduce down a third again, then remove from the heat and stir in the knob of butter.

Substitutions.

Vinegars

Use flavoured or quality vinegars in place of white wine in the basic recipe to add a more piquant quality to cream sauce. Substitute all the white wine with ¼ cup vinegar. Reduce the vinegar by half, then add cream and continue with the basic technique.

Try quality vinegars such as sherry, chardonnay, red wine and white wine vinegars. The better the quality of the vinegar, the better the taste of the sauce – with one exception. I do not recommend balsamic vinegar for cream sauce.

Liquors

The same rule that applies to vinegar also works with liquors. Substitute all the wine in the basic recipe with ¼ cup unsweetened spirits. Alternatively, replace the white wine in the basic recipe with the same amount of red wine, cider or champagne.

Use red liquors such as port and red wine as a sauce with red meat; white spirits such as vodka and gin in a sauce for fish; and champagne or cider with chicken. Spirits such as brandy and cognac are great with all meats.

Variations.

Pepper

White wine cream sauce can be flavoured with any coloured peppercorn, such as pickled green peppercorns, dried pink, or white or black. Always crush peppercorns before adding to the pan or pot to help release the flavours into the cream.

Use 1 tablespoon peppercorns to flavour the basic recipe and add at the beginning when the onions and garlic are sweated together. Suitable for all kinds of red meat as well as chicken, peppercorn white wine cream sauce is often used in the deglazing method after peppered meat has been cooked and removed from the pan.

Fresh tomato

Fresh tomato makes a delicious, slightly acidic, addition to cream sauce. The tomatoes need a little preparation to eliminate skin and seed from the sauce. Do this by making *tomato concasse*:

Remove the cores and blanch tomatoes in boiling water for about 30 seconds until the skin starts to peel off. Plunge tomatoes into iced water so they stop cooking instantly.

After 5 minutes remove tomatoes from the water and cut in half across the middle. Scoop out all the seeds and chop the tomato into a fine dice.

Add the chopped tomato to the finished cream sauce and simmer for 3 minutes before serving.

Use tomato cream sauce with chicken, fish and bacon. Herbs can also be added to this sauce (see Herbs).

Cheese
The 2 main cheeses used in cream sauces are Parmesan and blue cheese.

Parmesan – fresh Parmesan is generally added to any cream sauce for pasta. Don't add the Parmesan to the cream sauce while it is cooking as it may burn; instead I recommend grating the cheese over the pasta just before serving.

Blue cheese – add 60g blue cheese at the same time as the cream in the basic technique. As the cream reduces, the blue cheese has time to melt and flavour the cream. Blue cheese cream sauce is delicious with beef, chicken and bacon.

Saffron
When you add the wine to the basic recipe add a pinch of saffron for a bright yellow sauce that works well with chicken and bacon.

Mustard
Every type of mustard can be added to a white wine cream sauce. Add 1 tablespoon of mustard at the same time as the cream to flavour the basic recipe. Mustard cream sauces are primarily served with beef steaks, but are also well suited to lamb, venison and pork dishes.

Capers
Sweat 1 tablespoon caper buds with the onions and garlic, then continue with the basic recipe technique.

Herbs
Most herbs are suitable for white wine cream sauce. I recommend using just one herb variety at a time in cream sauce so the flavours don't become jumbled and the herb is clearly defined.

I would not recommend using mint, coriander and Vietnamese mint in cream sauces as the flavours are quite Asian, and this is not an Asian sauce. Add strong-flavoured herbs with tough fibre, such as thyme and rosemary, a few minutes before the sauce is finished to get maximum flavour into the sauce. The softer herbs such as basil, chervil and chives should be added when the sauce is finished and ready to serve. In this way the colours and flavours are not overcooked and ineffective.

Lemon
Add the grated zest of 1 lemon to the onions and garlic, then proceed with the technique as normal. Use lemon in white wine cream sauce to complement any kind of fish.

Avocado
When stirring in the butter at the end of making the sauce, add 1 peeled, deseeded and chopped avocado then gently heat through. Great with chicken, cured meats and bacon dishes, and also a tasty addition to pastas.

Mushroom

Add 150g of sliced button or flat mushrooms to the onions and garlic, then continue with the basic technique. Be careful not to mash the mushrooms with the spoon so they remain as intact as possible. Use mushroom sauce with chicken, beef and bacon.

Cucumber

Peel the skin from ½ a cucumber. Discard the green skin and continue to peel off the flesh down to the seeds. Discard the seeds, then add the ribbons to the basic recipe at the same time as adding the white wine. Continue with the basic technique. Use cucumber cream with fish dishes – it's especially good with salmon and capers.

Egg yolks

One of the most famous cream sauce dishes in the world is fettucine carbonara.

To make this delicious creamy pasta, sauté bacon strips with sliced button mushrooms in a little butter for about 5 minutes then pour on one quantity of the basic cream sauce.

Stir in cooked fettucine and heat through. Remove from the heat when bubbly hot and wait for the bubbling to stop.

Stir in 2 egg yolks until well incorporated into the cream sauce. The sauce will slightly thicken. Do not be tempted to return the sauce to the heat as the yolks will curdle. Serve immediately.

Innovations.

Sour cream

Sour cream can turn a cream sauce into an extra rich sauce.

Stir 4 tablespoons sour cream into the finished sauce, then heat through gently until just under boiling. Try sour cream and mushroom cream sauce for a rich, extra tasty combination.

Crème fraîche

Use crème fraîche in the same way as sour cream to finish a cream sauce. It has the advantage of not tasting as sour as sour cream but adds all the richness of a double cream flavour to the sauce.

Combination sauces

Combination sauces from the ingredients above can be tasty and exciting additions to your culinary repertoire. Pick only one or two flavours from each section to avoid flavour confusion, with the exception of lemon, herbs and pepper.

Here are some ideas to get you started:

+ Chardonnay vinegar, caper and chive cream sauce
+ Port wine, fresh tomato and rosemary cream sauce
+ White wine, lemon zest, cucumber and chervil cream sauce
+ Green peppercorn, whole seed mustard and brandy cream sauce

Smoked paprika seared chicken breast with pappardelle pasta, olives, rosemary and white wine cream sauce.

Serves 4

200g dried pappardelle (or other pasta)
1 quantity basic cream sauce (p.27)
90g quality black olives
2 tablespoons olive oil
4 tablespoons smoked paprika
2 teaspoons plain salt
400g boned and skinned chicken breast
1 spring onion
1 sprig rosemary, leaves picked off and chopped, for sauce and garnish
Parmesan, shaved, for garnish
Italian parsley leaves for garnish

Prep.

Cook the pasta in plenty of boiling water with 1 teaspoon salt added (about 9 minutes of simmering for dried pasta and 3 minutes for fresh).

Drain into a sieve and if not being served immediately toss with 1 teaspoon cooking oil to prevent sticking. If the pasta does stick, don't pull apart; simply run under a little water until the pasta loosens again.

Heat the cream sauce and the olives and half the rosemary leaves.

Add the pasta back into the cream sauce to heat through when ready to serve.

While the cream sauce is warming, heat the second tablespoon of oil in a frying pan.

On a plate mix the smoked paprika with the salt, then slice the chicken breast into thin slivers and place into the paprika mix. Cover the chicken completely in the spice and pat off the excess.

Fry the chicken on a medium heat for about 2 minutes, then turn over and fry for a further minute. Switch off the heat and allow the chicken to sit for a further 2 minutes to finish cooking through.

To serve.

Slice the spring onion on a diagonal as thinly as possible, then shave the Parmesan with a cheese shaver or vegetable peeler.

Carefully pour the pasta and sauce into a serving bowl and place the paprika chicken, sliced spring onion, rosemary, Parmesan and parsley leaves on top. Serve immediately, piping hot.

Wild mushroom spaghetti with white wine cream sauce, Parmesan and fresh thyme.

Serves 2

150g fresh assorted wild mushrooms
1 tablespoon olive oil
1 quantity basic cream sauce (p.27)
2 sprigs rosemary, leaves roughly chopped
200g fresh or dried spaghetti
1 sprig rosemary, leaves pulled off, for garnish
Parmesan, shaved, for garnish

Prep.

Bring a large pot of water to the boil.

In another large pot sweat the mushrooms in olive oil for around 1 minute until they soften a little, then drain on paper towels.

Heat the cream sauce and add the sautéed mushrooms and rosemary.

Meanwhile, cook the spaghetti in plenty of boiling water with 1 teaspoon salt added (about 9 minutes of simmering for dried pasta, 3 minutes for fresh).

Drain spaghetti into a sieve.

To serve.

Toss the spaghetti with the mushroom cream sauce. Ladle into 2 hot serving bowls and garnish with the rosemary leaves and shaved Parmesan. Serve immediately.

Smoked paprika seared chicken breast with pappardelle pasta, olives, rosemary and white wine cream sauce. p.29

Wild mushroom spaghetti with white wine cream sauce, Parmesan and fresh thyme. p.29

Mayonnaise and aïoli.

Mayonnaise is said to be the invention of the French chef of the Duc de Richelieu in the mid 1700s. While the Duc was defeating the British at Port Mahon, his chef was creating a victory feast that included a sauce of cream and eggs. When the chef realised that there was no cream in the kitchen he improvised, substituting oil for cream. A new culinary masterpiece was born, and the chef named it Mahonnaise in honour of the Duc's victory.

Mayonnaise is a semi-solid emulsion of vegetable oil and egg yolk with vinegar or lemon juice, seasoned with salt. Aïoli is the French word for garlic-flavoured mayonnaise and is sometimes referred to as the butter of Provence. Raw, peeled garlic can be used to make aïoli, but I prefer roasted garlic because the aïoli will be a little sweeter in flavour.

Still a mystery to many, mayonnaise is a quick, easy staple to have available in your refrigerator once you have mastered the art of emulsion. You may be surprised by the many variations possible.

For first-timers, make the basic recipe before attempting any variations in order to see how the sauce comes together. It is also advisable to hand whisk your first mayonnaise to see close up how the technique really works. Never overload the yolk mixture with more oil than can be whisked in as this will cause a split effect and ruin the sauce. No amount of whisking will make mayonnaise emulsify once a split has occurred.

If a split does occur, the ingredients need not be wasted. Save the mayonnaise by starting with a fresh egg yolk in a clean bowl or clean blender with a little water, then at a snail's pace pour the split mayonnaise onto the new yolk. If oil is left over from the previous attempt, add it to the new yolk then follow with the split mixture. Keep whisking until all the split mayonnaise has been whisked into the new yolk.

Basic mayonnaise recipe.

1 egg yolk
30ml white vinegar
1 teaspoon English mustard
⅔ teaspoon plain salt
1 cup soya bean or plain vegetable oil

Prep.

Place the egg yolk, vinegar, mustard and salt into a blender then switch on to high.

As slowly as possible (even if it takes 10 minutes) drizzle the oil into the blender, forming the thinnest stream possible, until all of the oil has been used up. It is crucial the oil is not added too fast, especially at the beginning as the emulsion that bonds oil with yolk can be broken this way.

After all the oil has been incorporated, a thick mayonnaise results.

If the mayonnaise is still very runny, it has split and will gradually separate back to the original form of oil and yolk. Refer to the introduction of this chapter for split mayonnaise advice.

Aïoli.

Heat the oven to 180°C. Toss 9 large cloves of peeled garlic lightly with vegetable oil, salt and pepper, wrap in foil and place on the bars in the oven. (Don't rest garlic on a solid surface or the base will burn.) Roast for 20 minutes.

When the garlic has cooled, add it to the basic recipe along with 2 teaspoons lemon juice before the oil is added, then add the oil using the same basic technique in a blender.

Substitutions.

Changing mayonnaise into a flowing dressing

For a thin tangy mayonnaise dressing, reduce the oil in the recipe to ¾ cup. Add 3 tablespoons lemon juice for a creamier, flowing dressing.

Citrus mayonnaise

Add 1 teaspoon grated lemon or lime zest to the basic recipe and omit the vinegar. Substitute the vinegar with lemon or lime juice for a citrus-flavoured mayonnaise.

Variations.

Caesar mayonnaise

Using the mayonnaise technique, before the emulsion is made by blending with the oil, add to the yolk mixture:

1 tablespoon capers, 1 tablespoon grated Parmesan, 1 tablespoon lime (or lemon) juice, 1 teaspoon anchovies, 2 minced cloves garlic and 1 tablespoon chopped parsley. Blend in the oil as usual.

Remoulade sauce

Using the mayonnaise technique, before the emulsion is made by blending with the oil, add to the yolk mixture:

1 chopped celery stick, 1 tablespoon chopped white onion, 1 minced clove garlic, 1 tablespoon horseradish cream, 1 tablespoon tomato paste, 2 teaspoons lemon juice, 2 teaspoons Cajun spice and 1 teaspoon paprika. Blend in the oil as usual.

Thousand Island dressing

Blend into the finished mayonnaise:

1 tablespoon tomato paste, 1 tablespoon horseradish (fresh or cream), 1 teaspoon Worcestershire sauce (Lea and Perrins), 2 teaspoons lemon juice, ¼ teaspoon paprika and 1 minced clove garlic.

Tartare sauce

Add the following chopped ingredients to the basic mayonnaise after blending:

1 large gherkin, 1 tablespoon capers, 1 tablespoon dill and 1 tablespoon lemon juice.

Chilli and lime mayonnaise

Add 2 teaspoons chilli sambal and ¼ teaspoon minced garlic to a lime mayonnaise. Chilli lime mayonnaise is sensational with luxury seafood such as crayfish, lobster, prawns and crab.

Herb mayonnaise

Use any herb to flavour mayonnaise but I prefer to keep flavours simple by just choosing one. Choose one herb that suits the dish with which the mayonnaise is to be served.

Fish: dill, chervil
Chicken: chives, basil
Lamb: rosemary, mint
Beef: thyme, rosemary or sage
Salmon: basil, chervil

The technique works well for any herb flavours. If the herbs are blended into the mayonnaise instead of chopped and added last, the flavour and colour is more evenly dispersed. Add the fresh herbs before blending in the oil. Use herb mayonnaise as a condiment with fried food, in salads and sandwiches, or as a sauce with a main course.

Innovations.

Ginger aïoli

Using the aïoli technique, add 60g peeled root ginger at the same time garlic is added to the recipe. Ginger aïoli makes a great dipping sauce for spicy marinated chicken and salmon kebabs.

Avocado mayonnaise

Blend the flesh of ½ a large avocado or 1 small avocado into the finished basic mayonnaise. The mayonnaise takes on the smooth creamy texture of the avocado as well as its gentle flavour.

Serve with mild-flavoured meats such as smoked chicken and anything with salmon.

Pimento mayonnaise

Heat the oven to 180°C. Cut 1 red capsicum in half and remove the seeds. Place it cut-side down on a shallow oven tray. Drizzle with a little olive oil and bake until the skin has wrinkled and the flesh is soft to the touch, approximately 20 minutes.

When cool, remove the skin and blend into 1 quantity of basic mayonnaise.

Serve pimento mayonnaise as a vegetable dip or a spread for breads.

Fruit in mayonnaise

I would not normally use fruit in mayonnaise, but there are a couple of exceptions to the rule, such as tamarillo and red plum.

The fruit needs to be poached briefly (see Poached Fruit, p.151), then drained, skinned and deseeded before being blended into the finished basic mayonnaise recipe. Use 2 tamarillos or 2 plums to flavour the mayonnaise and blend into the mayonnaise. Serve red fruit mayonnaise with meats that traditionally work well with sweet condiments, such as pork, duck and game meats.

Spices in mayonnaise

To add the flavour of dried spices to mayonnaise, roast 2 teaspoons of the seeds gently to release their flavour then allow to cool. (I usually only use one spice at a time.) Either add the whole seeds to the basic recipe before blending, or crush in a pestle until powdery then blend into the finished mayonnaise.

Some of my favourites are cumin seed, coriander seed (blended with fresh coriander or cilantro), smoked paprika (add ¼ teaspoon) and saffron. Heat the vinegar until it steams, soak a pinch of saffron in it for 15 minutes, then blend with mayonnaise as normal.

Lemon and coriander dressing

Use the basic flowing dressing technique. Omitting the vinegar and before drizzling in the oil, add 2 tablespoons fresh lemon juice (5 tablespoons in total), 1 teaspoon whole seed mustard, 2 teaspoons runny honey, 1 minced clove garlic and 1 bunch chopped fresh coriander or cilantro. This dressing suits seafood fritters, fried fish pieces, squid rings and Thai fish cakes.

Roasted cloves of garlic.

Prosciutto, bocconcini, red capsicums, black olives and baby spinach leaves with rosemary cream dressing. p.40

Green bean salad with gourmet potatoes, brown sugar glazed Spanish onions, soft-boiled eggs and anchovy dressing. p.41

Prosciutto, bocconcini, red capsicums, black olives and baby spinach leaves with rosemary cream dressing.

Serves 4 as a side dish

Bocconcini are small white balls of fresh mozzarella. Bland in flavour, they are the perfect accompaniment to stronger flavours and add a unique spongy texture to a dish.

For the dressing

1 egg yolk
½ teaspoon hot English mustard
30ml white wine vinegar
1 clove garlic
4 sprigs rosemary, leaves removed from stalk
½ teaspoon salt
pinch white pepper
¾ cup soya bean oil

Prep.

Place all ingredients except the oil in a blender. Blend in the oil as per the basic recipe technique.

Refrigerate, covered, until ready to serve.

For the salad

2 red capsicums
olive oil for drizzling
1 spring onion
6 balls bocconcini
6 slices prosciutto, rind removed
12 black olives
baby spinach leaves

Prep.

Heat the oven to 180°C. Cut the peppers in half and remove the seeds, then place cut-side down on a shallow oven tray. Drizzle with a little olive oil and bake in the oven until the skin has wrinkled and the flesh is soft to the touch, approximately 20 minutes.

Allow to cool then peel off the skin and cut in half again lengthways.

Slice the spring onion on an angle then sit in cold water to curl.

To assemble.

Roll the bocconcini up in the prosciutto and place on a serving platter.

Place the capsicums and olives between the rolls, then garnish with the spinach leaves, spring onion and rosemary cream dressing. Serve immediately.

Green bean salad with gourmet potatoes, brown sugar glazed Spanish onions, soft-boiled eggs and anchovy dressing.

Serves 2

Anchovy dressing
1 egg yolk
1 tablespoon white wine vinegar
3 tablespoons lemon juice
1 clove garlic
15g anchovies
1 teaspoon capers
1 teaspoon caper brine
1 teaspoon hot English mustard
1 level teaspoon salt
¾ cup soya bean oil

Prep.

Place all ingredients except the oil in a blender. Turn the blender on to high speed.

Pour in a steady but very thin stream of oil. When all the oil is used up, the result should be a thin tangy mayonnaise.

Refrigerate, covered, until required.

Brown sugar glazed onions
2 Spanish onions
1 tablespoon brown sugar
30ml balsamic vinegar

Preheat the oven to 180°C. Peel the onions and slice through the core into 8 wedges. Mix onions with the brown sugar and balsamic vinegar. Roast in a roasting pan for 20 minutes, tossing occasionally, then set aside until serving time.

Assembling the salad
500g gourmet potatoes
100g green beans
4 eggs soft boiled for 7 minutes then peeled
freshly ground black pepper

Place the potatoes in a medium-sized pot, cover with cold water and bring water to the boil. Turn down the heat and simmer until the potatoes are just cooked, about 15 minutes from when the water starts to simmer. Drain the potatoes and leave to cool while preparing the other vegetables.

Bring a medium-sized pot of water to the boil.

Trim the beans and cut them in half across their length. Blanch in the simmering water for 1 minute then plunge into iced water to rapidly cool.

To serve.

On a large serving platter layer the vegetables and sliced eggs then drizzle over a little of the dressing. Sprinkle with cracked black pepper and serve.

Vinaigrette.

In France the name for cold oil and vinegar salad dressing is vinaigrette. The western term for vinaigrette is French dressing, which became popular in Britain and America in the late 1800s. As salads became more common in the early 20th century, recipes for vinaigrette began to be published. Many derivatives have developed over the years, with emphasis on its use in green salads.

The type of dressing used with a salad is important to define the salad type. For example, a Caesar salad would not be a Caesar salad without a tasty anchovy and Parmesan vinaigrette enriched with egg yolks. Properly seasoned vinaigrette transforms everyday ingredients into a taste sensation. Season salad ingredients with a little salt and cracked black pepper after tossing through the vinaigrette, to ensure the salad's maximum flavour potential.

The quality of vinaigrette can be measured by the quality of the oil and vinegar used. For the best vinaigrette use good quality wine vinegar (either red or white) that is not overly strong and biting. The best imported French, Spanish or Italian wine vinegars contribute the best flavour to vinaigrette and, if available, are well worth a little extra money.

Before discussing the different ways to flavour vinaigrettes, it is important to cover the basics of ratio and ingredients. Vinaigrette is made up primarily of 2 ingredients: oil and vinegar. The ratio is 1 part vinegar to 3 parts oil. This means if you make vinaigrette with 1 cup of oil, use ⅓ cup of vinegar.

Here is the basic recipe for an unflavoured vinaigrette. This recipe makes a tasty vinaigrette to use in salads as it is, without flavouring in any way.

Basic vinaigrette recipe.

Makes 1½ cups of vinaigrette

1 cup oil
⅓ cup vinegar
2 teaspoons Dijon mustard
1 large clove garlic, minced
½ teaspoon plain salt
½ teaspoon white sugar
freshly ground black pepper

Prep.

While the ingredients can be whisked together, I recommend blending all ingredients in a blender to bring together a part emulsion. This leaves the vinaigrette thick enough to coat the back of a spoon and creamy in texture.

Substitutions.

Substitute the oil

Now to play with the flavours. I use olive oil or vegetable oil. If I use olive oil, it is only with a strong acidic flavour, such as lemon juice or balsamic vinegar. These simple vinaigrettes are seasoned only with salt and milled pepper. They are not blended and stay separated after being lightly whisked together. Strong in flavour, they are also quick to make. Other ingredients can easily be overpowered by olive oil so restrict your expensive oil to distinct simple combinations.

Vegetable oil that isn't too strongly flavoured is best for vinaigrette, such as soya bean, sunflower or canola oil. As another option, use these cheaper oils as a base then add a strong-flavoured oil to the vinaigrette. For a sesame vinaigrette, replace 1 tablespoon of the vegetable oil with 1 tablespoon of sesame oil. As a guide, here are some strong-flavoured oils to mix with vegetable oil to flavour vinaigrette:

+ **Chilli oil**
+ **Truffle oil**
+ **Sesame oil**
+ **Coconut oil**

The cheaper vegetable oils can be replaced completely with a slightly more expensive oil that gives a different flavour, for example:

+ **Avocado oil** (use as you would olive oil)
+ **Peanut oil**
+ **Hazelnut oil**
+ **Sunflower seed oil**
+ **Walnut oil**
+ **Wheatgerm oil**
+ **Grape seed oil**
+ **Citrus-infused olive oils**

In addition, don't forget those delicious home-made infusions of herbs and garlic.

Substitute the vinegar

The next part of the vinaigrette is the acidic part. In the basic recipe for vinaigrette, I have used vinegar, but here are some other examples of tasty acidic bases that can be cut 50/50 with vinegar:

+ **Lemon juice**
+ **Grapefruit juice**
+ **50/50 lemon and orange juice**
+ **Lime juice**
+ **Soy sauce**
+ **Add grated zest of any citrus fruit used for extra flavour**

Vinegars – where do I begin? I cannot think of a vinegar not suitable for vinaigrette. Try vinegars you haven't used before and experiment, particularly with the most common vinegars, to become familiar with the different flavours, for example:

+ **Cider vinegar**
+ **Red wine vinegar**
+ **Sherry vinegar**
+ **Chardonnay vinegar**
+ **Herb-infused vinegar**
+ **Rice wine vinegar**

Obviously not every combination will work in an amazing fashion – trial and error is what learning is all about, so here are some great combinations I know will work for you:

+ **Lemon juice/lemon-infused olive oil/fresh tarragon**
+ **Rice wine vinegar/peanut oil/soy sauce/honey/sesame oil**
+ **Red wine vinegar/rosemary-infused olive oil**
+ **Sherry vinegar/walnut oil**

Variations.

While I can't cover every variation of vinaigrettes, here are the basic additions generally made to flavour a salad or meat course in traditional and innovative ways.

Egg yolks

The classic way to enrich vinaigrette is with egg yolks. While the ingredients are the same, this is not a mayonnaise due to the different quantities of ingredients and the method. The classic example is the Caesar salad:

Whisk 2 egg yolks, 2 tablespoons finely grated Parmesan and 1 teaspoon anchovy paste into a half quantity of basic vinaigrette. For the salad, toss the dressing with cos lettuce leaves, croûtons, sliced spring onions and grated Parmesan just before serving.

Cheese

The most famous vinaigrette cheese used is without a doubt blue cheese. Due to the creamy thick texture the blended blue cheese gives the vinaigrette, the name is changed to blue cheese dressing. Make the basic vinaigrette recipe, then add 90g of your favourite blue cheese and blend in a liquidiser until smooth.

Tomatoes

Tomato concasse is made by removing the skins of tomatoes by blanching with boiling water, removing the eye and seeds then chopping the tomato into a fine dice. For tomato vinaigrette that suits fish or salads, whisk in tomato concasse made from 3 large tomatoes and 1 teaspoon tomato paste added to the basic vinaigrette recipe.

Spices

Not many spices are suitable for vinaigrettes, but some can give a great effect in addition to other flavours. Spices worth trying include saffron, paprika, turmeric and different-coloured peppercorns. For a spicy chilli vinaigrette, add 1 chopped red chilli and 1 teaspoon paprika to the basic vinaigrette.

Curry powder

Curry powder adds a fantastic colour and flavour to vinaigrettes. Do not blend this vinaigrette. Substitute the vinegar in the basic recipe with balsamic vinegar. Add 1 skinned, deseeded and chopped mango, 1 tablespoon curry powder and 1 small, finely chopped white or red onion for a spicy, delicious vinaigrette that works incredibly well with chicken.

Green herb
In a liquidiser blend the basic vinaigrette with a large bunch of your favourite green herb (stems removed) such as basil, tarragon, parsley, coriander, mint, chives or rosemary. A herb vinaigrette will only stay bright green for one day so stick to the hard leaf herbs such as rosemary, thyme and sage if you need longevity.

Use herb vinaigrettes with summer salads, meat and hot vegetable dishes with appropriate herbs such as chervil and dill for fish, basil and coriander for chicken, and rosemary and thyme for red meats.

Mustard
For a really mustardy vinaigrette, triple the mustard in the basic recipe using either reconstituted mustard powder, honey-cured mustard seeds, hot English or extra Dijon mustard. For a honey mustard dressing, add 1 tablespoon runny honey to the basic recipe as well as the extra mustard. Mustard vinaigrettes suit red meat, salmon and chicken.

When using wholegrain mustard, hand whisk the oil onto the other ingredients so the grains remain intact.

Innovations.

Sesame
Before blending, add to the basic recipe: 2 teaspoons sesame oil, 2 tablespoons soy sauce, 2 teaspoons runny honey. Blend as usual then stir in 2 tablespoons toasted sesame seeds.

Japanese
Do you enjoy the tasty side salad served in Japanese restaurants? The ratios for this dressing are a little different from vinaigrette but here is my version of the recipe. Serve tossed through frizzy lettuce, sliced iceberg lettuce and sliced white cabbage.

Stir together in a bowl: 2 tablespoons peanut oil, 2 tablespoons rice vinegar (substitute with white wine vinegar if not available), 2 tablespoons pickled ginger brine, 20g chopped pickled ginger, 20g minced shallot or white onion, ⅛ teaspoon salt and ⅛ teaspoon sesame oil.

Smoked salmon and avocado salad with pecorino cheese, baby cos leaves and roasted tomato vinaigrette.

Serves 4 as a side dish

Pecorino is a Parmesan-style cheese made from ewe's milk. It is very strong in flavour and should be served lightly shaved as overloading with the flavour can be unpleasant. I have used salty salmon and bland creamy avocado to offset the strong cheese flavour of the pecorino. Finish off the combination with a sweet and sour tomato vinaigrette, which supplies the acid needed for a tasty salad.

Roasted tomato vinaigrette
2 large tomatoes
2 tablespoons olive oil
1 tablespoon white wine vinegar
½ teaspoon caster sugar
¼ teaspoon plain salt
freshly ground black pepper

Prep.

Preheat the oven to 180°C.

Slice the tomatoes in half through their sides so that all the segments inside are exposed, then scoop out the seeds. Place them cut-side down in a small baking dish and roast for 10–12 minutes. They will be soft to prod when cooked properly.

Remove tomatoes from the oven and when cooled peel off the skins reserving the leftover tomato juices. Chop tomatoes until very fine then add the tomato juices back into the chopped tomatoes.

Stir in the vinegar, sugar, salt and pepper.

Smoked salmon salad
baby cos lettuce leaves
1 spring onion
1 avocado
pecorino cheese for shaving
250g sliced cold smoked salmon

Wash the cos leaves and leave to drain while preparing the other ingredients.

Slice the spring onion on a very sharp angle, then leave in cool water for a few minutes to curl.

Peel and deseed the avocado, then cut into fine slices.

Shave the cheese with a cheese shaver or peeler.

On a serving dish layer half the ingredients starting with the cos, avocado, smoked salmon, spring onion and shaved pecorino, then drizzle with some of the vinaigrette. Repeat the process until all of the ingredients have been used up.

Rare seared eye fillet with mung bean salad and ginger sweet and sour vinaigrette.

Serves 4 as an entrée

Vinaigrette
¼ cup soya bean oil
2 tablespoons soy sauce
2 tablespoons balsamic vinegar
1 tablespoon sweet chilli sauce
½ teaspoon sesame oil
¼ teaspoon plain salt
½ small red onion, minced
½ tablespoon minced ginger root
½ tablespoon minced garlic
1 tablespoon minced coriander stalk

Prep.

In a small mixing bowl stir together the above ingredients until just combined. This can be prepared a long time in advance and should have no problem lasting in the refrigerator for up to a month.

Seared eye fillet
2 tablespoons cooking oil
4 x 100g slices eye fillet

Heat a medium-sized frying pan and oil until the oil just starts to smoke. Carefully place the fillet pieces in the oil and sear for about 2 minutes before turning and repeating on the other side. If you enjoy steak cooked a little more then leave it in longer.

Remove the steak from the pan and allow to rest on paper towels for a minute before serving.

Mung sprout salad
½ packet mung bean sprouts
coriander leaves
1 spring onion

Slice the coriander leaves into strips and place in a mixing bowl with the mung beans. Slice the spring onion on a very sharp angle and add to the bowl.

Gently toss together.

To serve.

Mix a little of the vinaigrette into the mung bean salad and divide salad between 4 serving plates.

Slice each piece of warm fillet into 8 pieces (helps the vinaigrette flavour to pierce the beef) and place on serving plates next to the salads.

Spoon some of the vinaigrette over the beef, making sure there are plenty of vegetable bits from the dressing for maximum flavour.

Smoked salmon and avocado salad with pecorino cheese, baby cos leaves and roasted tomato vinaigrette. p.48

Rare seared eye fillet with mung bean salad and ginger sweet and sour vinaigrette. p.49

Pesto and Pistou.

It is always handy to know the basics of quick sauces made without heating for a meal in a hurry. Pesto and pistou are simple sauces that only require the ingredients to be popped into the blender, whizzed, and served. The shelf life of these sauces is considerable, at least two weeks. However, I like to make these sauces when I need them in order to maintain the freshest flavour and colour in the sauce.

Firstly, the definition of these sauces and what makes them different from one another.

Pesto
One of the most famous Italian sauces in the world would have to be pesto. Pesto is made from blending herbs, nuts, fresh garlic and olive oil to a thick paste then seasoning with lemon juice and salt. The main ingredients are fresh basil leaves and pine nuts. If the herbs and nuts are changed to other varieties, purists insist it is no longer pesto. But the technique is the same and the word pesto is retained to explain which technique and what additions have been used to make a herb and nut paste.

Pistou
Pistou is a French variation of pesto that has the same ingredients minus the nuts. The amounts of ingredients are adjusted to give a smooth green paste despite missing the bulk of the nuts. A fantastic option for people with nut allergies, and also a cheaper option, pistou makes a great sauce for pastas, salads and meats.

It is common to add Parmesan to both sauces during the blending, but I never add it as I don't like the flavour it contributes to the recipe. I would rather shave fresh Parmesan onto the finished dish for a fresher flavour. I also object to blended Parmesan soaked in oil sitting the fridge while the pesto is stored, as the freshness of the cheese is even more impaired with time.

Use both sauces tossed through pasta, or for vegetable dips and meat sauces. While primarily a summer sauce due to seasonal herbs, there are some winter options. I like pesto well seasoned with extra citrus as my basic recipe reflects.

Basic pesto recipe.

60g pine nuts
60g fresh basil leaves (no stalks)
1 tablespoon lemon juice
¼ cup olive oil
1 clove garlic
¾ teaspoon salt

Prep.

Lightly toast the pine nuts for around 10 minutes in an oven preheated to 150°C and then leave to cool. It is very important the nuts are cooled or the heat from them will cook the basil, ruining the colour and texture.

Place the nuts in a blender with the basil leaves, lemon juice, olive oil, garlic and salt, then blend on high until the mixture turns into a paste. Transfer to a bowl, cover with cling film and chill.

Basic pistou recipe.

60g basil leaves (no stalks)
½ cup olive oil
1 tablespoon lemon juice
⅓ teaspoon salt
1 small clove garlic

Prep.

Place the above ingredients in a blender and blend on high for several minutes until the basil has turned to a fine purée.

Scrape down the sides of the blender and pulse the blender again to ensure even blending.

Transfer to a bowl, cover with cling film and chill.

Substitutions.

Technically, pesto is not pesto without basil leaves and pine nuts. Nevertheless, the technique works so well with other ingredients that it is hard not to play with the endless options available. Soft leaf herbs work best in blended sauces. While thyme and rosemary can be used, they are a little more difficult to work with and a lot harsher in flavour. It pays to use them 50/50 with another herb, for example basil or parsley, and sharp blender blades are a must.

Flat leaf parsley

While curly parsley can be used for pesto, it requires a blender with extremely sharp blender blades. I don't enjoy the consistency in the end product as much as with Italian or flat leaf parsley. Remove most of the end stalks as they are a little tough for blending. The stalks nearer the leaves are softer and can blend into the sauce more easily. Parsley is as versatile as basil and suits any kind of meat, fish or vegetarian meal.

Mint

Mint-flavoured pesto works a treat as a sauce with a lamb dish. It can also work with chicken as a cooling agent if you flavour chicken in a lime and chilli marinade. Mint pistou complements hot and spicy nibbles very well as a dipping sauce. Try a combination of coriander and mint pistou as a sauce with spicy Thai meals to add a cool freshness. Remove all the mint's stalks before puréeing.

Fresh rocquette leaves.

Porchini mushrooms.

Toasted pinenuts.

Mortar and pestle.

Dill
Only use dill pesto with fish dishes. It is very strong in flavour and doesn't suit vegetarian or meat dishes all that well. Having said that, it is fantastic on fish and makes a lovely pistou sauce. Use with freshwater fish such as trout and salmon, or exotic seafood and white fish. It also makes a great condiment on seafood platters as a dipping sauce and works a treat dotted onto seafood pastas made with tomato-based sauces. Remove stalks from the dill leaves before puréeing.

Coriander
If you enjoy the flavour of coriander, you will love it in pesto. Remove the root then purée the leaves and stalks into the pesto after chopping quite fine. Coriander is a strong-flavoured herb, so use coriander pesto as a sauce to complement chicken, duck, salmon and pork. As a pistou, it also works well with fish as a dipping sauce, and both sauces complement vegetarian food with an aromatic burst of flavour.

Oregano
A strong-flavoured herb such as oregano is best used with chicken and red meat. Experiment with the stronger-flavoured nuts such as walnuts, Brazils and pine nuts. The stalks can be tough so remove first. Enjoy this aromatic herb in a sauce with Mediterranean-style salads and pasta dishes, or as a dip for breads.

Roquette
Land cress or roquette leaves are slightly bitter and peppery making a bright green, slightly spicy pesto. The leaves break down easily in the blender and the colour lasts for a considerable amount of time. Depending on the nut used, roquette suits any kind of meat and is great in salads and pastas. Slice off any stalks as they can strangle the blender blade.

Watercress
Watercress is similar to roquette only even more peppery. The stalks are soft, so chop them quite fine and they will blend into the sauce. Watercress pistou is a tasty sauce option for all exotic and regular seafood as well as freshwater fish. Use it for the most expensive seafood purchases such as prawns, crayfish and crab as the perfect complement.

Nuts that sit around in your pantry for too long can turn rancid. Always taste the nuts before using to check for any unpleasant or bitter flavour. Don't use any nuts that are not perfect as any unpleasant flavour will taint the delicate sauce.

Variations.

Substitute any of the following nuts with the pine nuts in the basic pesto recipe. Make sure they are unsalted, raw and preferably skinless as the skins can be bitter. I have added some variations that work well with appropriate combinations, so enjoy experimenting in the summer.

Cashew nuts
The perfect partner for coriander, use cashews with all the herbs except dill. Mild in flavour, they mash nicely into the sauce leaving a creamy consistency. Coriander and cashew nut pesto makes an outstanding combination with brie and camembert cheese.

Skinned peanuts
Only use skinned peanuts with coriander – there is too much flavour confusion with other herbs as peanuts are so overpowering.

Almonds
Almonds are a great substitute for pine nuts with basil, and a lot cheaper as well. Use whole blanched almonds so there are no husks. I also recommend almonds with watercress and roquette pesto. They have the mildest flavour and will complement any of the herbs.

Macadamia nuts
Blanched macadamias are also mild in flavour and will complement any of the herbs as well. I love them in mint pesto.

Brazil nuts
Any herb goes well with Brazil nuts except for dill. They make a tasty pesto for every meat but avoid using with fish.

Hazelnuts
There are not many options for hazelnuts as they are also strong in flavour. Try them with parsley, roquette and watercress for an extra nutty flavour. Serve hazelnut pesto with red meats and game.

Pistachios
Use pistachios with any of the herbs except mint and dill. They are one of my favourite nuts and work extremely well in pesto. As pistachios are Middle Eastern, for something a little different try flat leaf parsley pesto with 1 teaspoon roasted ground cumin seeds. Substitute the lemon juice with red wine vinegar for a tasty and piquant sauce with spiced red meats.

Walnuts
The strongest-flavoured nuts are walnuts and pecans. Use walnuts with basil, parsley, oregano, watercress and roquette for sauces that suit chicken, game, red meat and pork.

Sunflower seeds
Not technically nuts, sunflower seeds are an interesting idea for pesto. A great option for people with nut allergies, although please check first. They are suitable with any herb and quite mild in flavour.

While all these recipes require olive oil as the binding agent, additional flavour can be added through adding either infused olive oils or other vegetable oils.

Sesame oil
Sesame oil is an Asian ingredient so I recommend it with the coriander and cashew nut pesto. Add ½ teaspoon sesame oil and ½ teaspoon red curry paste for an all-round Asian-flavoured pesto with a serious bite. Substitute peanut oil with olive oil for an additional flavour. Serve Asian coriander pesto with salmon and chicken.

Walnut oil
An expensive oil, but it adds a delicious buttery flavour to a walnut-based pesto. Alternatively, use walnut oil for a walnut-flavoured pistou without using the actual nuts. Substitute half the olive oil with walnut oil.

Chilli oil
Add ½ teaspoon chilli oil for an extra bite to a peppery-based pesto or pistou. Ideal with watercress and roquette-based sauces and a strong enough flavour to complement red meat such as beef, venison and lamb.

Lemon-infused olive oil
Anything lemony suits chicken, lamb and fish. Purchase lemon-infused olive oil or infuse your own as a cheaper option. Substitute the entire regular olive oil in the basic pistou recipe with lemon-infused olive oil. Try lemon oil and dill with fish, lemon oil and basil with chicken, or lemon oil and oregano with lamb.

White cheese pasta with roasted olives, capsicums and basil pistou. p.60

Salmon carpaccio with dill pistou, chilli, cucumber and lime salsa. p.61

White cheese pasta with roasted olives, capsicums and basil pistou.

Serves 4

I have used ewe's milk cheese for this recipe but use your own favourite soft white cheese. I recommend goat's feta, goat's cheese, cow's feta or bocconcini. I really enjoy the flavour of roasted olives as I think they take on an entirely different flavour from raw. The olive oil they are roasted in can also be kept and used in dressings or to roast capsicums or where an extra olive flavour boost goes well.

Use any pasta you like for this salad, except avoid long stringy pasta such as spaghetti as eating becomes a bit messy. For the purpose of a cold pasta salad, stick with smaller sizes that can catch the sauce. I used seashell pasta for this recipe.

For the salad
2 red capsicums
olive oil for drizzling
2 cups pasta
1 teaspoon salt
1 avocado
12 black olives
60g sliced ewe's milk cheese
1 quantity basil pistou (p.54)

Prep.

Heat the oven to 180°C.

Cut the capsicums in half, remove the seeds and place cut-side down on a shallow oven tray. Drizzle with a little olive oil and bake in the oven until the skin has wrinkled and the flesh is soft to the touch, approximately 20 minutes. When the capsicums have cooled, remove skin and slice into quarters.

Cook the pasta in plenty of simmering water with the salt (about 9 minutes of simmering for dried pasta and 3 minutes for fresh pasta).

Drain the pasta into a sieve and if not being served immediately toss with 1 teaspoon cooking oil to prevent sticking. If the pasta does stick don't pull apart; simply run under a little water and it will loosen again.

Cut the avocado in half then remove the seed and skin. Slice the avocado into slices across the width.

To assemble.

Layer all the ingredients into a serving bowl starting with the pasta, then the capsicums, cheese, olives, avocados and pistou, until all the ingredients have been used.

Salmon carpaccio with dill pistou, chilli, cucumber and lime salsa.

Serves 2

250g pink boned salmon fillet from the thick end
1 red chilli
zest and juice of **1** lime
1 tablespoon olive oil
½ telegraph cucumber
¼ **teaspoon** salt
freshly ground black pepper
½ **quantity** dill pistou (p.54)
extra sprigs dill

Prep.

To prepare the salmon

Make sure the salmon is absolutely free of all skin, bones, scales and fat, then slice across the grain of the fish on the sharpest possible angle. Each piece needs to be flattened out between 2 sheets of baking or wax paper. Do this by using a mallet, the edge of a rolling pin or a meat tenderiser on the flat side. Gently pat the fish and slowly flatten it working from the inside to the outside until the fillet is around twice the length and width. Avoid making holes – you may need 2 pieces per person.

The fish can be stored like this, between the papers, until ready to serve. If storing overnight, wrap in cling film as well to avoid drying out.

To prepare the salsa

Remove all seeds and white pith from the chilli, then finely dice and place in a mixing bowl with the lime zest, lime juice and olive oil.

Slice the cucumber in half along the length then scoop out the seeds. If not using a telegraph cucumber, peel off the skin as well. Dice the cucumber and add to the mixing bowl.

Stir the ingredients together, then cover with cling film and refrigerate until ready to serve.

To serve.

Decide which side of the salmon is the most attractive and remove the paper from the other side by peeling it away at a sharp angle.

Place the paperless side on 2 plates and peel away the top layer of paper. Repair any holes by pushing the flesh together to give the salmon a seamless look.

Sprinkle the vegetable salsa evenly over the salmon, including any remaining juice. Season well with salt and cracked black pepper. Dot with the dill pistou. Place the sprigs of dill evenly over the salmon. Serve immediately.

Fish & Meat.

03

Hot smoking fish and vegetables.

Foods have been preserved by smoke curing since before the dawn of recorded history. Throughout the world all cultures have relied on smoke-curing fish and meat products for long-term storage.

The most primitive form of smoking meat involved slicing meat into strips and hanging over an open fire to dry. The smoke sealed the outer layer of meat leaving a protective skin.

In Britain and Europe during the Middle Ages, various heavily smoked and salted foods carried people over the lean times of late winter and into spring. Fresh fish could not be transported any distance from the port of landing unless preserved.

Nowadays we rely on freezing and refrigeration for preserving so smoking plays a minor role in cuisine and is largely used just for flavouring, with the obvious exception of ham. A combination of brining and smoking is used to turn pork meat into ham, and is the most common smoked food available on the market.

Smoking can be separated into two categories: cold smoking and hot smoking. Cold smoking is the technique used to preserve smoked salmon, purchased vacuum-packed and sliced very thin. Cold smoking does not cook the fish, instead smoke without heat circulates the hanging fish, flavouring it and preserving it without heat. Usually a fire is kept alight in one room, and the smoke is forced into a second room where the meat hangs to avoid contact with heat. The process takes many hours, sometimes days, and a lot of equipment, so I will concentrate on the speedy technique of hot smoking.

Hot smoking is easier if you have a small smoker, available from barbecue shops. Otherwise use an old pot you don't mind getting a little dirty. (Refer to the basic recipe for instructions on how to construct a makeshift smoker on p.68). You need some untanalised woodchips or bark, also available at barbeque shops. The only thing left to consider now is flavouring the meat. As mentioned in the brining section, p.80, brining was used to prepare meat for the smoker, so any recipe in that section is ideal for preparing fish and will retain more moisture than an instant marinade. But as that takes planning ahead, the focus here is on quick methods of preparing meat for smoking.

The smoke from a smoker can leave a bitter aftertaste in fish and vegetables. Also, blandness is a problem with subtly flavoured fish, so two ingredients are added as a seasoning to counter this: sugar to balance the bitterness and salt for flavour. A problem with sugar is its quality of melting as the crystals dissolve in the heat, so as thick a paste as possible is made to stop the seasoning sliding off the smoked item. As a liquid is needed to make a paste from the sugar, use soy sauce so the salt and water are contained in one ingredient.

Smoked chillies.

Prepared capsicums.

Wood chips.

Smoked olives.

Smoker.

Basic smoking marinade recipe.

60g soft brown sugar
1 tablespoon soy sauce

Prep.

Mix together the sugar and soy sauce to form a thick paste. Brush onto meat or vegetables then place into smoker.

Grease the racks in the smoker well with oil to prevent the food sticking.

For a makeshift smoker

60g brown sugar
60g uncooked rice
4 teabags or **4 teaspoons** tea
¼ cup water

If bark and a smoker are not available, here is an easy replacement using things already in your kitchen.

Mix the above ingredients together (take tea out of bags and discard bags) and line a heavy-based pot with foil. Place the tea mixture into the pot (I use a steamer) and make sure none of the tea touches the actual pot as it is difficult to clean off.

Place the food to be smoked in the steamer basket and place basket in the pot. Cover with a tight-fitting lid or cover with tightly wrapped foil. Switch the extractor fan on to high. Place the makeshift smoker on a high heat, then when you see smoke appear turn down the heat to low. Smoke the food until cooked.

Substitutions.

Substitute the sugar

Use liquid sugars such as maple syrup, treacle, molasses and golden syrup. Instead of using soy sauce, add 1 level teaspoon salt to 60g sugary syrup. Heat the liquid sugars gently in the microwave until they are runny enough to work with, then stir in the salt and brush onto the food. If the syrup becomes overheated and too runny, let it stand and cool until thick enough.

Substitute the sugar and soy sauce

It is worth mentioning a thick sweet soy sauce called kecap manis. Because it already has the sugar and salt in it, kecap manis makes the perfect instant seasoning for all smoked foods.

Variations.

Smoked freshwater fish

Trout and salmon are simply delicious when hot smoked. Do not cook them all the way through, but gently smoke so they are moist in the middle and the flesh flakes away easily. Grease the racks well to prevent sticking. Check the fish after 10 minutes of smoking – they may require another 5 minutes depending on the temperature of the smoker. Larger pieces can be served as a main course; smaller pieces for starters, or used in salads and pastas.

Smoked white fish

Smoking white fish is a little trickier. Use thick pieces of even thickness as overcooking will dry the fish and it needs to be cooked evenly. Avoid thin fillets such as tarakihi, gurnard and cod as they dry out too easily. Use thick fillets of snapper, hapuka or marlin. Alternatively, smaller fish such as mullet can be smoked whole. Skin the fish and brush the flesh with marinade, also brushing the marinade into the gut cavity. Perfect as a main course, or use in salads, chowder or other fish soups.

Smoked shellfish

Mussels, pipis and cockles all smoke well. Steam open first, then smoke for 10 minutes to flavour. Ideally marinate after smoking to prevent from drying out.

Tomatoes

Remove the eyes from the tomatoes and slice through their sides so all the segments are exposed. Brush with the marinade and smoke for 15 minutes. If smoking meat, put tomatoes in the smoker as well to serve on the side or to use as a flavouring for mayonnaise, to blend into vinaigrettes or other sauces, or to toss in salads and pasta – just about anything really!

Innovations.

Capsicums

Instead of charring or roasting capsicums, smoking adds a delicious flavour while cooking. Use red capsicums for smoking as they keep their attractive colour, then toss in salads, pastas and stir-fries for an extra flavour boost. Smoke for 15 minutes.

Garlic

Toss garlic lightly in smoking marinade then drain. Lay garlic on a piece of foil just big enough to contain it then smoke until soft, about 15 minutes. Fantastic for flavouring cream sauces, tossing in salads and for smoked garlic aïoli.

Eggplant

Cut eggplant in half lengthways and score with a knife almost to the skin. Salt heavily and drain for 15 minutes. Wash eggplant then dry with paper towels and brush with marinade. Smoke until the flesh is soft all the way through. This can take up to 30 minutes, depending on smoker temperature. Purée with olive oil, garlic and lemon juice for a delicious smoked eggplant dip.

Chillies

Smoking chillies only takes about 10–15 minutes. Toss chillies in the marinade, then drain and place on a piece of foil just big enough to contain them and smoke. Add to salads; serve fried with meats; or add to smoked tomato ketchup for an extra piquant barbecue sauce.

Smoked mussels in a chilli and garlic marinade. p.71

Smoked mussels in a chilli and garlic marinade.

Serves 4

½ small white onion, peeled
1 cup white wine
20 large live mussels in their shells
1 large clove garlic, peeled
1 chilli
2 tablespoons roughly chopped coriander
1 tablespoon olive oil
1 tablespoon sweet chilli sauce

Prep.

Roughly slice the onion and place in a large pot with the wine and mussels on a high heat. Cover and stir occasionally.

As the mussels open, pull them out to cool. If any refuse to open, discard them as they could be risky to eat.

Smoke the mussels for 10 minutes in a smoker then set aside to cool.

Slice the clove of garlic into thin rounds and roughly chop the chilli. Sprinkle over the mussels.

Stir in the coriander, olive oil and sweet chilli sauce then refrigerate, tightly covered, until serving time.

Another option is to prepare the marinade in advance and serve with smoked mussels hot from the smoker.

Smoked tomato ketchup.

1 tablespoon soy sauce
60g soft brown sugar
4 large tomatoes
1 peeled white onion, roughly chopped
2 cloves garlic, peeled and roughly chopped
1 teaspoon cooking oil
1½ teaspoons plain salt

Prep.

Make a paste from the soy sauce and brown sugar.

Remove the core from the tomatoes and cut in half through the side. Place cut-side up on a workbench and pile the sugar paste high on the tomatoes, then smoke for 15 minutes.

Sweat the onions and garlic in the oil for about 3 minutes then add tomatoes and salt, and simmer together for 20 minutes.

Purée the sauce then pass through a fine sieve.

This sauce has the shelf life of a week and is fantastic with stronger-flavoured meats. It can also be frozen. Try using this ketchup at your next barbecue!

Slow-cooked meats.

Braising and stewing are almost identical methods of cooking, except that stewing involves the use of more liquid and the meat and vegetables are cut into smaller-sized pieces. Braising is generally used for larger cuts such as chops and shanks, and is done in the oven in a deep roasting tray where there is more room for the bone-in cuts.

Braising and stewing is designed to tenderise tougher cuts of meats that are inedible by other cooking methods. Do not use lean cuts of meat for stewing and braising, such as tenderloins, as they have a tendency to dry out from the lengthy cooking time. In the past meat was placed in liquid and put on to heat with the vegetables. Nowadays meat is lightly fried before being placed in the water to stew in order to retain the nutritious juices and help colour the gravy.

Stews and casseroles derive from cooler countries where fire or coal ranges were kept alight all day to warm a house or just one room. Tough cuts of meat could be slowly simmered over a gentle heat with vegetables until tender. Originally, open fire was used and a pot dangled over the fire but later ceramic casserole dishes were placed into a coal range, the first ovens used in England and France.

Stews are served as winter fare to warm the body on a cold night. They are a traditional comfort food but there is plenty of room for innovation. New variations can be made using favourite ingredients and experimenting with different meat cuts and other vegetables.

Serve stews piping hot with boiled new potatoes, mashed potatoes, lentils or steamed white or brown rice.

Common stewing terms.

Stew
usually has vegetables and/or dumplings cooked with the meat.

Haricot
is a stew with the meat and vegetables cut into very fine, small pieces.

Ragout
is a wine-based stew.

Salmi
is a stew based on game meat.

Chowder
is a fish stew.

Fricassee
is meat stewed and served in a white stock sauce.

Braising
is a slow cooking method of uniform heat within a confined space.

Basic stew recipe.

Serves 4

2 tablespoons cooking oil
800g meat cut into cubes
1 white onion, peeled
3 sticks celery, washed
1 carrot, peeled
8 cloves garlic, peeled and halved
750ml white or red wine
150ml water
1 teaspoon chopped thyme
¼ cup white wine or red wine vinegar
1 teaspoon white sugar
1½ teaspoons salt
2 tablespoons soft butter
2 tablespoons flour
chopped flat leaf or curly parsley

Prep.

Heat the oil in a frying pan and colour the diced meat over a strong heat for 8–10 minutes. Place the meat in a pot that holds at least 6 litres of liquid.

Chop the onion, celery and carrot into large dice and fry with the garlic in the same pan for 2–3 minutes.

Place the vegetables on top of the meat in the pot. Pour over the wine and top up with water to cover the meat. Add the thyme and bring to a simmer. Cover with a lid and simmer on low until the meat is cooked and tender. (See Variations for different meat cooking times.)

When the meat is cooked, skim off any fat that has risen to the surface. Add the vinegar, sugar and salt to the pot.

Mix together the butter and flour to a smooth paste. Using a balloon whisk, make a well in the centre of the pot clear of meat and vegetables. Scoop up the butter paste onto the whisk and gently whisk into the wine stock in the pot.

Whisk gently until there are no lumps, then simmer for a further 5 minutes.

Sprinkle with chopped parsley and serve.

Variations.

Chicken

For boneless diced chicken in a stew, allow 25 minutes simmering to cook the meat through.

A whole chicken cut into 10 pieces only requires 35 minutes simmering.

Frozen chicken pieces require 1 hour of simmering. Thaw properly before cooking or the cooking time can be affected.

Cook turkey or rabbit meat for the same length of time as chicken.

Beef

For diced beef, allow 1½–2 hours cooking time. Check by cutting into a piece to make sure the meat flakes apart easily before adding the seasonings and finishing the stew. Cook venison for the same length of time as beef.

Pork

For boneless diced pork meat, simmer for 1½ hours until tender. Use white wine and white stock bases for pork to preserve the delicate flavour. Pork stews are also a great way to cook any type of pork chops.

Lamb

Diced lamb takes about 1 hour of simmering to cook, especially if using tender leg meat. Alternatively, simmer the whole leg in the liquid for 2 hours then carve the meat to serve. Lamb meat works particularly well with cream in stews.

For an Irish stew, cover diced lamb with water and bring to the boil. Simmer for 30 minutes then remove the meat and strain the stock.

Add gourmet potatoes to the stock and simmer for 15 minutes. Add baby carrots, sliced washed leeks, sliced celery and the meat back into the stock and simmer for a further 5 minutes.

Pour in 1 cup cream and simmer for a further 10 minutes.

Stir in 1 teaspoon salt and top with chopped parsley.

Mash some of the potatoes into the cream stock for a thicker stew, or use the basic technique thickening method. I prefer it without either.

Lamb shanks

Roughly chop 2 carrots, 1 peeled onion and 6 celery sticks. Place vegetables into a deep-sided baking tray.

Sear lamb shanks in a frying pan with hot oil on both sides until nicely browned. Place seared shanks on top of the vegetables in the baking tray.

Bring equal quantities of red wine and beef stock to a simmer. (Powdered stock and water works fine as a substitute for beef stock.) Pour the hot stock over the shanks until covered up to two-thirds and season with salt, black pepper and chopped thyme.

Cover tightly with foil and braise in the oven for 2 hours.

After braising, strain off the liquor, skim off the fat, and reduce liquor by simmering until it becomes a thick sticky sauce.

Quickly reheat the shanks in the sauce and serve.

Ham hocks

Heat the oven to 180°C. Place the hocks in a deep-sided baking tray.

Heat the cooking liquor to a simmer – use stock, apple juice or a stock and white wine combination. Pour over the hocks until two-thirds covered. You can add spices that suit pork to the cooking liquor, for example cinnamon, cloves and allspice. Cover tightly with foil and place in the oven.

Cook raw hocks for 2½ hours; smoked hocks for 1½–2 hours.

After braising, strain off the liquor, skim off the fat, and reduce liquor by simmering until it becomes a thick sticky sauce.

When cooled a little, remove the skin and bones from the hocks (optional).

Quickly reheat the hock meat in the sauce and serve.

Carbohydrates in stews for a total meal

The most common carbohydrate used in stews is potato. Add 500g peeled and diced potatoes to the basic recipe 30 minutes before the finished cooking time. Other options include lentils, beans, chickpeas, barley and even rice. For each stew, select one of these options to avoid flavour confusion and add ½ a cup to the stew when the wine is added. Chickpeas and legumes need to be soaked for 2 hours, overnight if possible, before being added to the stew. They also require 1½–2 hours of simmering to cook, so cook separately and add at the end if making a chicken or quick-cooking meat stew.

Vegetables

There are many options for vegetables in stews. Add tomatoes, capsicums and mushrooms when the wine is added to the pot at the beginning of cooking time.

For starchy vegetables such as potatoes, parsnip, okra, kumara and pumpkin, add 30 minutes before the end of cooking time to ensure they don't overcook and break up.

Add vegetables such as corn, peas and diced eggplant 10 minutes before the end of the cooking time so they don't lose too much flavour and colour.

Salted flavours

To capture the flavour of the Mediterranean in a stew, use olives, capers, lemon zest and anchovies in addition to herbs such as marjoram, basil and oregano. The salty flavours can go in the stew at the beginning of cooking time. Add fresh herbs just before serving.

Dumplings

Dumplings are best cooked by the steam from the stew. It is not necessary to immerse them in the liquid. Place on top of the meat and vegetables so the steam reaches them. The pot must be covered while the dumplings are in, and the stew should be served as soon as they are cooked or they may become heavy and waterlogged.

250g plain flour
1 teaspoon salt
2 teaspoons baking powder
2 tablespoons olive oil
150ml milk
4 tablespoons chopped fresh flat leaf parsley (optional)
4 tablespoons chopped fresh chives (optional)
extra flour for dusting

Sift the flour, salt and baking powder into a large bowl. Make a well in the centre and add the olive oil and herbs.

Pour in the milk and mix to form a soft dough with a fork.

Place the dough on a lightly floured surface and knead briefly. Divide and shape into 16 teaspoon-sized dumplings.

Place the dumplings on the surface of the casserole 35 minutes before the stew is cooked and cover with a lid.

The dumplings and meat should finish cooking at the same time.

Coq au vin.

Serves 2–4

1 whole size13 chicken
1 tablespoon cooking oil
2 tablespoons flour
10 rashers streaky bacon
12 baby onions, peeled
12 button mushrooms, washed
8 cloves garlic, peeled and sliced in half
750ml red wine
1 teaspoon chopped thyme
¼ cup malt or red wine vinegar
1 teaspoon white sugar
1½ teaspoons salt
2 tablespoons soft butter
2 tablespoons flour
flat leaf or curly parsley, chopped

Prep.

Cut the chicken in half through the breastbone. Cut away the rib bones and remove the spine. Chop off the leg and last wing joint. Cut out the thighbone (connects the knee to the thigh). Cut the breast into 3 pieces and the leg into 2 pieces. There should now be 10 pieces of chicken.

Heat the cooking oil in a frying pan until it just starts to smoke.

Dust the chicken pieces lightly with flour and sear in oil until golden brown. Place chicken in a pot that can hold at least 6 litres of liquid.

Roll up the bacon rashers tightly, place in the frying pan and fry until golden brown. They will tighten as they cook, keeping their shape. Add the bacon to the chicken in the pot.

Add the onions and mushrooms to the frying pan and continue cooking over a slow heat until onions are a little soft and start to brown.

Add the garlic to the frying pan, cook for 2 more minutes then add all the vegetables to the chicken pot.

Pour the wine into the pot and top up with water so all the ingredients are covered. Sprinkle on the thyme and bring to a simmer. Skim the surface every 10 minutes to remove any scum.

Simmer for about 35–45 minutes or until the chicken is tender.

Add the vinegar, sugar and salt to the pot.

Mix together the butter and flour to a smooth paste. Using a balloon whisk, make a well in the centre of the pot clear of chicken and vegetables. Scoop up the butter paste onto the whisk and gently whisk into the red wine stock in the pot.

Whisk gently until there are no lumps, then simmer for a further 5 minutes.

To serve.
Sprinkle with chopped parsley and serve.

Mediterranean pork stew.

Serves 3–4

3 tablespoons cooking oil
800g boneless diced pork meat
10 peeled baby onions, quartered
3 celery sticks, washed and sliced
8 cloves garlic, peeled and sliced in half
1 red capsicum, deseeded and sliced
1 yellow capsicum, deseeded and sliced
12 black olives
12 green olives
4 anchovies
zest of **2** lemons
12 caper berries
2 tomatoes, cored and chopped
750ml white wine
1 teaspoon chopped oregano
¼ cup white wine vinegar
1 teaspoon white sugar
1½ teaspoons salt
2 tablespoons soft butter
2 tablespoons flour
extra whole oregano leaves

Prep.

Heat a frying pan with 1 tablespoon olive oil until it just starts to smoke. Sear half the pork lightly in the oil until golden brown.

Place pork in a pot that can hold at least 6 litres of liquid. Repeat the process with the other half of the pork.

Heat another tablespoon of oil in the frying pan then add the onions and celery. Cook for a couple of minutes over a slow heat until onions are a little soft and start to brown.

Add the garlic to the frying pan, cook for 2 more minutes, then add the vegetables to the pork pot.

Heat the last tablespoon of olive oil in the frying pan and sear the capsicums for 3 minutes until they soften. Add the capsicums to the pot with all the olives, anchovies, lemon zest, caper berries, tomatoes and wine. Top up with water so all ingredients are covered, sprinkle with chopped oregano and bring to the boil. Skim the surface every 10 minutes to remove any scum.

Simmer on top of the stove for about 1½ hours or until the pork is tender.

Add the vinegar, sugar and salt to the pot.

Mix together the butter and flour to a smooth paste. Using a balloon whisk, make a well in the centre of the pot clear of pork and vegetables. Scoop up the butter paste onto the whisk and gently whisk into the white wine stock in the pot.

Whisk gently until there are no lumps then simmer for a further 5 minutes.

To serve.
Sprinkle with the whole oregano leaves and serve.

Coq au vin. p.76

Mediterranean pork stew. p.77

Brining meats.

Brining is a technique used to help retain meat juices and add flavour to white meats such as poultry, fish and pork products. Poultry and pork products dry out when cooked as the water content in the meat evaporates in the heat. Often confused with marinating and curing, brining originally involved soaking meat in a sugar and salt solution for a limited time before washing the meat, leaving it to air dry then smoking it.

Air drying helped form a protective skin over the meat that kept out impurities and so better preserving the meat.

Today only a small amount of food is preserved through the brining technique in this country. It is largely only used for curing hams, but can add a huge amount of flavour and tenderness to barbecued, roasted and pan-fried meats. Different brines for different meats as well as flavouring brines are explained here. If you haven't tried this technique yet, have a go as only a little time and some salty water is required to make tasty changes and improve on the meat's texture.

While the basic recipe technique is fine to use on its own for meat to be brined, I have included ideas for flavouring brine for unmarinated meat. Brine flavouring must be very strong as the meat is patted dry of brine before cooking to reduce saltiness. The brining process will stop once the meat is removed from the brine, so when the time is up pat the meat dry and refrigerate until cooking time.

Definition of brining

When meat is placed in brine, the meat's cell fluids are less concentrated than the salt water in the brining solution. Water flows out of the cells in the meat and salt flows in. The salt then dissolves some of the fibre proteins, and the meat's cell fluids become more concentrated, thus drawing water back in. When the meat is cooked it is still able to retain a high moisture content and becomes moist, juicy and tender. The meat is also well seasoned with salt so no additional seasoning is required at cooking time.

Basic meat brine recipe.

Serves up to 8 people

¼ cup plain salt (not iodised)
¼ cup white sugar
1 litre water

Prep.

Bring the above ingredients to a simmer in a large pot and stir a few times until all the sugar and salt has dissolved.

Switch off the heat and cool to room temperature.

Stored in an airtight container in the refrigerator, this brine will keep indefinitely.

Always discard the brine after use as the meat juices could contaminate the new meat used.

The basic brine recipe is enough to cover a whole chicken in a watertight bag. Use 4 times the recipe for a turkey and half the recipe for chops or chicken pieces. If brining pork roast, remove the skin for crackling as it won't crisp properly if brined. Roast the crackling separately.

Basic fish brine recipe.

Serves up to 4 people

¼ cup salt
¼ cup sugar
½ cup water

Prep.

Bring the above ingredients to a simmer in a large pot and stir a few times until all the sugar and salt has dissolved.

Switch off the heat and cool to room temperature.

Timing

Brine boneless meat and fish for 12 hours. Brine meat on the bone for 24 hours. Place the meat or fish in a leak-free plastic bag and cover in brine. Secure bag with a string tied tightly into a knot then shake until all the meat is covered with brine. Turn the meat once during brining for maximum coverage.

Always pat the meat or fish dry with paper towels before cooking to ensure a minimum of salt in the flesh. If you really object to salt, wash thoroughly then pat dry before cooking.

Roast whole birds in an oven bag to avoid the skin burning.

Cider cranberry glaze. p.88

Pickled green peppercorns.

Juniper berries.

Star anise.

Treacle and thyme brined salmon.

Substitutions.

Substitute the water

Apple juice

Substitute the water completely with apple juice or cider for an apple-flavoured brine. Fantastic with pork, turkey, chicken and duck.

Orange juice

Use filtered fresh orange juice mixed with apple juice – 3 parts apple juice to 1 part orange juice. Grated or peeled zest of oranges will also add substantial orange flavour to the brine. Suitable for pork, duck and chicken.

Lemon juice

Substitute ½ cup water from the basic recipe with filtered lemon juice. Grated or peeled zest of lemons will also add substantial lemon flavour to the brine. Makes a tangy quick brine suitable for chicken and fish.

Stock

Use vegetable or chicken stock in place of the water for a tastier brine in all meats, but not good with fish.

Soy sauce

Substitute 100ml water with soy sauce. Perfect with chicken for an Asian-inspired version and works outstandingly well with Szechwan peppercorns and star anise.

Coconut cream

Substitute half the water in the basic recipe with coconut cream. Flavour with ginger and garlic for brining white fish and chicken.

Substitute the sugar

Brown sugar

Brown sugar has more of a caramel flavour than white sugar and will also add an attractive caramel colour to the meat.

Maple syrup

While this is an expensive option it is also a tasty one. Substitute the full quantity of sugar in the basic recipe with ½ cup maple syrup. Works well in brine for fish as the flavour is more concentrated.

Molasses and treacle

For a strong sugar flavour, substitute the sugar with treacle or molasses. I recommend only substituting half the sugar with molasses as it is extra strong, but treacle is very tasty as a total substitution.

Variations.

Spices

Any of the following spices are worth experimenting with in brine. Add the spice of choice to the liquid before it is boiled to infuse the flavour. Don't forget that the brine is thrown away before the meat is cooked, so don't use ingredients you can't bear to see go down the drain. Few spices are strong enough in flavour to carry over into the finished product, but the following spices do have enough kick to taste the meat after cooking:

+ Peppercorns
+ Juniper berries
+ Star anise
+ Cumin seeds
+ Cayenne pepper
+ Allspice
+ Saffron

Garlic

Flavour any brine with garlic by peeling and slicing 6 large cloves and adding to the brine before it is heated. The flavour of the meat after cooking is of cooked garlic, so don't worry about the garlic flavour being too intense. I suggest adding the pieces of garlic to the oven bag, or putting the garlic inside the cavity of whole birds to continue flavouring the meat through the cooking process.

Root ginger

Ginger also works well with any brine, especially a soy sauce brine. Slice 60g peeled ginger and add to the brine before boiling. Add pieces of ginger to the oven bag, or put the ginger inside the cavity of whole birds to continue flavouring the meat through the cooking process.

Herb additions

The only herbs with a strong enough flavour to stand out in brine are rosemary, tarragon and thyme. Add the chopped herb of your choice to the brine at the end of cooking when the brine is still hot.

Innovations.

For meat cooked straight from the brine, it is worth experimenting and finding your own flavour combinations. Here are a few ideas to get you started:

+ **Duck:** orange juice, apple juice, juniper berry, thyme and treacle brine
+ **Chicken:** lemon juice, lemon zest, garlic and tarragon brine
+ **Salmon:** treacle and fresh thyme brine
+ **White fish:** lime juice, brown sugar and ginger brine
+ **Pork:** apple juice, garlic, black pepper and clove brine

Roast turkey with prune and cashew stuffing with cider cranberry glaze. p.88

Balsamic brined pork chops with pickled baby beets and radish. p.89

Roast turkey with prune and cashew stuffing with cider cranberry glaze.

Serves up to 8 people

Cranberry cider glaze

170g craisins or dried cranberries
1 litre apple cider
2 tablespoons white sugar
zest and juice of **1** orange

Prep.

Place all the above ingredients in a medium-sized pot, bring to the boil then turn down to a simmer. Simmer the liquid gently until it reduces to 500ml.

Cool to room temperature then refrigerate until serving time.

As an option, reheat the sauce and serve it hot.

Stuffing and roasting the turkey

6 slices bread
1 small white onion, peeled
70g cashew pieces
100g chopped prunes
50g butter
1 teaspoon chopped thyme
1 teaspoon dried sage
½ teaspoon salt
2 eggs
4.5kg whole turkey, brined for 24 hours in apple and star anise brine (4 litres of brine is needed to cover a turkey)

Preheat oven to 160°C. Rip the bread into small pieces in a large mixing bowl. Dice the onion very fine and add to the bread. Add the cashews and prunes.

Chop the butter very finely and add to the bowl with the herbs, salt and eggs. Stir together until combined.

Stuff the turkey cavity with the stuffing, pressing it in very firmly. Fasten the cavity with a couple of toothpicks to keep the stuffing in place.

Place the turkey in a large oven bag and fasten tight. Roast in the oven for 2 hours.

When cooked, let the turkey rest in the bag for 15 minutes before carving to allow the juices to settle.

To serve.

Carve and serve with the cranberry cider glaze.

Balsamic brined pork chops with pickled baby beets and radish.

Serves 4

What is the difference between pork meat and ham? Ham has been brined before smoking. If you enjoy eating ham but don't enjoy the gamey flavour of roast pork and pork chops, try this recipe. With the addition of vinegar, pickling brine puts an even bigger flavour boost into the pork chops while helping to cut out the gamey flavour. Use the pickling brine to prepare meat to be pan-fried or barbecued.

Balsamic brine for pork chops
500ml water
⅛ cup plain salt
⅛ cup soft brown sugar
⅛ cup balsamic vinegar
2 tablespoons cooking oil
600g pork steak medallions or chops
2 pears
50g blue cheese
50g chopped walnuts

Place water, salt, sugar and balsamic vinegar in a medium-sized pot. Bring to a simmer, stirring occasionally. Turn off the heat and let the brine cool to room temperature.

Place the pork chops in a deep-sided dish, cover with the brine and refrigerate, covered, for 12 hours, then remove from the brine and pat dry.

To prepare the beetroot
1 can baby beetroot
2 tablespoons white wine vinegar

Strain the beetroot juice into a medium-sized pot. Add the vinegar and bring to the boil, reducing down to 50ml.

Add the baby beetroot to the pot and switch off the heat until required.

Prep.

Place a medium-sized frying pan on a high heat and add the oil. When the pan starts to smoke, add half the pork chops and sear for 3 minutes. Don't shake the pan or move the chops around as they won't sear properly.

Flip the chops and sear the other side for another 3 minutes or until cooked through, then remove to a paper towel.

Repeat the process with the remaining chops.

To serve.

Wash and slice the pears. Place the pork (off centre) onto 4 warm plates, then stack with slices of beetroot and pear next to it. Crumble the blue cheese and chopped walnuts over the beetroot and pear.

Drizzle the salad with the beetroot vinegar and serve.

Vegetarian.

04

Polenta is the Italian word for cornmeal. The earliest Italians mixed water with kernels of wild grasses, pounded the mixture into a paste, then it was dropped onto hot stones and cooked like a tortilla. They also made polenta from a primitive form of wheat or chickpea flour. A hot porridge was made by mixing flour with water, or the flour was hardened into a cake and served cut into slices.

Millet and spelt were used next, to be replaced by barley. This was soon substituted with a far tastier grain, corn, after 1492 when Columbus returned to Europe from the New World. Corn was grown in northern Italy and soon took over as the primary polenta ingredient, becoming an important staple that is still preferred in many places to bread and pasta. Once considered a peasant food, polenta features regularly in many households and upmarket restaurants around the world and still dominates all aspects of modern and traditional Italian cooking.

Serve polenta either hot and creamy like mashed potatoes, or hardened into a cake and fried in pieces until crispy. Used as the starch accompaniment to a main meal, I prefer a softer, creamier texture and have included both versions.

Although polenta was originally made with water, it is extremely bland this way. Like most grain-based dishes, it needs to be flavoured heavily with other ingredients in order to gain the maximum flavour necessary to complement a dish. Garlic and Parmesan are used along with chicken stock instead of water. For a vegetarian option, use vegetable stocks and powders. If using a stock powder, the salt in the basic recipe will need to be reduced by half.

Polenta cake needs to be seared in a hot, oiled pan to be crispy, and it also deep-fries very well. After the cake is pressed into a dish, it needs chilling for about 3 hours to harden, then cut it into shapes and fry. Fried polenta is tasty tossed in a little Parmesan, just on its own, or served with vegetables in a salad. It makes a great hors-d'oeuvre when cut small, or cut larger pieces and serve with a main course. Serve creamy wet polenta with any dish instead of potato mash.

Polenta.

Basic polenta cake recipe.

Serves 4

Purchase finely ground polenta for this recipe, *not* coarse-ground.

700ml vegetable boullion or chicken stock
350ml cream
1 large clove garlic, minced
1½ teaspoons salt
50g finely grated Parmesan
300g finely ground cornmeal

Prep.

Bring the stock, cream, garlic and salt to a simmer.

In a separate bowl, mix the cornmeal and Parmesan.

Take the stock off the heat.

Holding a whisk in one hand and the bowl of polenta in the other, whisk the cream very quickly while 'raining' in the polenta mix. Whisk very fast as the mixture will thicken quickly.

Place the mix back onto a low heat and cook, stirring occasionally, for a further 10 minutes with a wooden spoon.

Turn the mixture out onto a shallow oiled tray and press evenly into the tray. Smooth the mixture so it is flat and tightly compacted, about a centimetre high. If the tray is too big, shape an edge with a palette knife.

Refrigerate for at least an hour before serving.

Creamy wet polenta.

700ml vegetable boullion or chicken stock
350ml cream
2 large cloves garlic, minced
1½ teaspoons salt
50g finely grated Parmesan
150g finely ground cornmeal

Prep.

Bring the stock, cream, garlic and salt to a simmer.

In a separate bowl, mix the cornmeal and the Parmesan.

Take the stock off the heat.

Holding a whisk in one hand and the bowl of polenta in the other, whisk the cream very quickly while raining in the polenta mix. Whisk very fast as the mixture will thicken quickly.

Place the mix back onto a low heat and cook, stirring occasionally, for a further 10 minutes. Serve immediately.

Substitutions.

Roast garlic

Heat the oven to 180°C. Peel 9 large cloves of garlic, toss lightly in cooking oil and wrap in foil. Place on the bars in the oven. Don't rest garlic on a solid surface or the base will burn. Roast for 20 minutes.

Mash the garlic roughly with a fork and add the paste to the stock, replacing the fresh garlic. Proceed as per the basic recipe technique.

Cheese

Replace Parmesan with blue cheese, Cheddar, smoked Cheddar or feta to flavour the polenta, or add a different cheese in addition to the Parmesan.

White wine

Substitute half the stock with white wine for a richer-tasting polenta cake.

Variations.

Black pepper

Milled black pepper is an interesting flavour addition to polenta. Add 1½ tablespoons to the hot liquid before whisking in the dry ingredients for a tasty peppery option.

Herbs

To flavour a polenta with herbs use the firm leaf varieties that are strong enough to flavour after a length of cooking. I would only recommend rosemary and thyme, as other softer herbs lose colour and flavour too quickly. Add destalked and chopped rosemary or thyme to the liquid in the basic recipe before the dry ingredients are added.

Mushroom

500g button mushrooms
2 tablespoons olive oil

Wash the mushrooms lightly to remove any dirt particles. Dry by brushing lightly with a paper towel. Slice off the stalk then slice the mushrooms as finely as you can.

Heat the oil in a frying pan. Add the mushrooms and sauté until soft and cooked through. Set aside until serving time.

When the polenta has finished cooking, stir in the mushrooms and continue with basic recipe instructions.

Innovations.

Anchovy

Anchovies take on an interesting salty flavour when cooked. They lose the fishy flavour which evaporates when heated. Most people who don't enjoy anchovies like the flavour of a dish with anchovies cooked into it. This is because a rich salty flavour is all that is left, with none of the unpleasant fur or bones so many people dislike. Add 4 roughly chopped anchovies to the liquid before heating, then proceed with the basic recipe technique. Anchovy polenta cake works particularly well as an hors-d'oeuvre with the addition of mayonnaise or aïoli as a dipping sauce.

Pumpkin
500g pumpkin skinned, deseeded and cubed
2 tablespoons olive oil
pinch ground nutmeg
pinch ground cinnamon

Line a baking dish with non-stick baking paper and add the pumpkin. Drizzle with olive oil and sprinkle with nutmeg and cinnamon.

Bake in the oven until the pumpkin is very soft without having browned too much, about 30 minutes. Cool pumpkin then crumble it gently.

Bring the cream, chicken stock, garlic and salt in the basic recipe, with the pumpkin, to a simmer. Add the dry ingredients and continue with the basic recipe.

Dried mushrooms
Heat the stock until simmering on its own in a pot. Remove from heat and soak 100g dried mushrooms in the stock for 20 minutes. Add the cream, garlic and salt, then bring to a simmer again and proceed as per the basic recipe technique.

Smoked paprika
Smoked paprika is the one spice I think suits polenta very well, giving it a slight chilli flavour. Serve smoked paprika polenta with any kind of vegetarian or meat dish, but it is especially good with smoked meats.

Add 1 tablespoon of smoked paprika to the stock and cream at the same time as the garlic and salt, then proceed as per the basic recipe technique.

Spinach and feta polenta with roasted black olives and sage butter.

Serves 4

100g freshly picked spinach leaves
3 tablespoons olive oil
1 quantity basic wet polenta
1 extra tablespoon olive oil
25 Kalamata olives
fresh sage leaves
100g feta

Prep.

Place the spinach leaves into a blender and blend on high speed. Add 3 tablespoons of olive oil, one spoonful at a time.

Set aside the spinach purée in a dish suitable for microwave and prepare the polenta.

While the polenta is cooking, heat the extra tablespoon of oil in a frying pan. Add the olives and fry on a low heat for 5 minutes. Toss in the sage and fry for an additional 2 minutes to flavour the olives.

Pour the cooked wet polenta into 4 warm serving bowls.

Heat the spinach purée in the microwave on high for 30 seconds. Dot the polenta with a little spinach purée and crumble on some feta. Working the fork in circles partially fold in the spinach and feta.

Top with the fried sage and olives and serve as a main course with a green side salad.

Roast pumpkin polenta cake salad with artichokes and caper berries, and trellis cream dressing.

Serves 2 as a meal

Sour cream dressing

100g sour cream
juice and zest of **1** medium-sized lemon
2 teaspoons white wine vinegar
2 tablespoons water
½ teaspoon salt

Combine all ingredients, cover with cling film and refrigerate until required.

To assemble the salad.

Use half a quantity of pumpkin polenta cake turned out onto a shallow oiled tray and pressed evenly into the tray. Refrigerate the cake until firm for about 2–3 hours.

2 tablespoons cooking oil
4 canned artichokes
6 trellis tomatoes
20 caper berries
fresh watercress leaves
olive oil for drizzling

Prep.

Turn out the polenta cake and cut into squares and then into triangles.

Heat the cooking oil in a frying pan and fry the polenta on a medium heat for about 4 minutes on both sides until golden brown. Drain on paper towels.

Slice the artichokes into quarters.

Slice the tomatoes in half through the sides.

To serve.

Arrange the polenta cakes, artichokes, caper berries and watercress attractively onto a serving plate. Spoon over the sour cream dressing and drizzle with a little olive oil.

Spinach and feta polenta with roasted black olives and sage butter. p.96

Roast pumpkin polenta cake salad with artichokes and caper berries, and trellis cream dressing. p.97

Risotto.

Most people consider risotto to be an intimidating and difficult recipe to follow. There are many variations on techniques for cooking risotto, but for beginners I recommend this simple, professional, no-fuss technique that steams the rice granules evenly, leaving you free to concentrate on other things.

All these recipes work well if the rice is continuously stirred for 20–25 minutes in a pan on the stove top. Use a heavy-based pot to avoid the rice sticking to the pan. When making the traditional Spanish dish paella, it is necessary to use a continual stirring technique as assorted seafoods are added at different stages of cooking.

While it is possible to use plain short grain rice to make risotto, the end effect is never as good. The cheaper rice does not have the capacity to hold as much liquid as the preferred rice, and the end product will be more like a light fried rice texture, or the rice will overload with liquid and the granules will fall apart. A properly made risotto using Arborio rice can hold a thick sauce with individually firm rice granules.

In the following basic recipe, there are two stages of cooking. After the first stage, if the rice is rapidly cooled it can be refrigerated then reheated with the remaining wine and cream when ready to serve. This cuts the preparation time in half at the time of serving.

The ideas for vegetarian risotto are seemingly endless. Substitute chicken stock with mushroom or vegetable stock to make a totally vegetarian dish. Alternatively, risotto works well as an accompaniment to a main course of meat or a small entrée with delicate seafood.

The options for risotto don't stop here. It makes great hors-d'oeuvres if given a coating of breadcrumbs and deep-fried – perfect for using up leftovers. Serve fried risotto balls with any chutney or relish for a tasty treat. Larger crumbed risotto balls make a tasty crumbed croquette which can be served as a main course with your favourite sauce. Risotto is incredibly tasty, versatile and vegetarian. Enjoy!

Aborio rice.

Basic risotto recipe.

600ml vegetable boullion or chicken stock
2 tablespoons cooking oil
150g white onions, peeled
1 clove garlic, peeled and minced
250g Arborio or short grain rice
1 teaspoon salt
200ml white wine
200ml cream

Prep.

Preheat the oven to 180°C.

Bring the chicken stock to the boil in a medium-sized pot.

In a separate large ovenproof pot, add oil and sweat the onions and garlic until soft on a low heat for about 5 minutes. Make sure the onions do not brown or get any colour on them.

Add the rice to the onions and stir continuously for a further 4 minutes.

Pour on the boiling chicken stock and bring the mixture back to the boil. Cover with an ovenproof lid or tightly with foil and bake in the oven for exactly 12 minutes.

When the rice is removed from the oven, it is ready to be flavoured. At this point it can be cooled with occasional stirring and reheated with the flavouring at serving time. When serving, bring the wine and cream to the boil then stir in the rice and salt.

Simmer until the cream has been absorbed.

Variations.

Pumpkin

Cut 300g raw peeled and deseeded pumpkin into cubes. Roast at 180°C with 2 tablespoons butter for approximately 30 minutes or until the pumpkin is soft. It will need to be turned at least 3 times while roasting. Allow to cool then purée in the blender on high until smooth. Refrigerate until required. Heat the pumpkin with the wine and cream, then stir into the rice and allow the liquid to be absorbed.

Saffron (risotto Milanese)

Soak 1 pinch saffron in 3 tablespoons hot water for 20 minutes. Add to the rice before steaming.

Lemon

Add the grated zest of 2 lemons at the same time as the rice is added to the stock.

Spinach

⅓ cup olive oil
90g freshly picked spinach leaves
½ teaspoon plain salt

Purée together the olive oil, spinach and salt until a smooth green paste is formed. After the cream has been absorbed into the rice, stir in the green paste and quickly bring to the boil. Serve immediately to preserve the bright green colour.

Porcini mushroom
Soak 90g dried porcini mushrooms in 200ml warm water for 20 minutes. Substitute one-third of the stock with the mushroom water and add to the rice at the same time (with the mushrooms) as the stock.

Flat or button mushroom
While sweating the garlic and onions, add 90g fresh sliced mushrooms and proceed as per the basic recipe technique.

Innovations.

Avocado
After the cream has been absorbed into the rice, add 1 ripe mashed avocado and bring the rice back to a simmer. Serve immediately to preserve the bright green colour and fresh flavour.

Florence fennel bulb and lemon
Add the grated zest of 2 lemons and diced fennel (recipe below) to the rice before steaming. Substitute half the stock with the fennel liquor.

1 Florence fennel bulb
1 small white onion, peeled
200ml white wine
600ml water

Preheat the oven to 180°C. Clean the fennel bulb under running water, remove the green leaves then slice into quarters through the length. Place into an ovenproof ceramic baking dish or a small stainless-steel deep roasting tray. Peel and roughly slice the onion, toss with the fennel and cover with the wine and water. Tightly wrap the dish in foil and bake in the oven for 40 minutes. Remove from the oven and set aside. Keep the liquid for the risotto. If the liquid has evaporated more than 300ml then top up with water.

Green pea
250g peas, blanched
90ml olive oil
½ teaspoon salt

Blend the peas with the olive oil and salt until puréed to a smooth paste.

After the cream has been absorbed into the rice, stir in the green paste and quickly bring to the boil. Serve immediately to preserve the bright green colour.

Watercress
¼ cup olive oil
200g freshly picked watercress leaves
½ teaspoon plain salt

Purée together the olive oil, watercress and salt until you have a smooth green paste. After the cream has been absorbed into the rice, stir in the green paste and quickly bring to the boil. Serve immediately to preserve the bright green colour.

Paella.

Serves 6

1.2 litres chicken stock
1 tablespoon butter
1 small white onion, peeled and finely chopped
1 large clove garlic, peeled and minced
1 Spanish chorizo, sliced
200g sliced (as in stir-fry) chicken
½ teaspoon paprika
1 large pinch saffron soaked in **1 tablespoon** hot water for 20 minutes
2 cups Arborio rice
4 mussels
4 pipis
1 squid tube, sliced
12 shelled prawns
12 scallops
⅔ teaspoon salt (if using a dried stock cube, reduce salt to **⅓ teaspoon**)
basil leaves for garnish

Prep.

Heat the stock in a pot to a slow simmer.

Melt the butter in a large heavy-based pot. Stir in the onion and garlic and cook gently for 2 minutes without colouring.

Add the sliced chorizo, chicken, paprika and saffron, then stir gently for another 2 minutes. Stir in the rice.

Add ¼ of the stock and when it simmers turn the heat down to low. Continue stirring continuously to avoid sticking and allow the liquid to cook into the rice.

Pour in another ¼ of the stock and when simmering add the mussels and pipis.

When the liquid is almost gone add another ¼ of the stock, then add squid and stir continuously.

When the liquid has reduced, add remainder of stock, the prawns and scallops and stir until the liquid is almost cooked into the rice. Add salt.

To serve.

Serve paella immediately in hot bowls, garnished with fresh basil leaves.

Roasted eggplant risotto with trellis tomatoes, goat's feta and oregano.

Serves 4

1 eggplant
2 tablespoons salt
2 tablespoons olive oil
600ml vegetable boullion
150g white onions, peeled
1 clove garlic, peeled and minced
2 tablespoons cooking oil
250g Arborio or short grain rice
4 trellis tomatoes
1 tablespoon olive oil
200ml white wine
200ml cream
1 teaspoon salt
100g goat's feta
fresh oregano leaves
olive oil for drizzling

Prep.

Heat the oven to 180°C. Cut the eggplant in half down the length and score the flesh down to (but not through) the skin. Rub the salt into the score marks and leave to drain in a colander for 15 minutes. Wash the eggplant well and pat dry. Place in a baking dish and drizzle with olive oil. Roast in the oven for 40 minutes.

Bring the chicken stock to the boil in a pot.

In a separate large ovenproof pot, sweat the onions and garlic in the cooking oil until soft on a low heat for about 5 minutes. Make sure the onions do not brown or get any colour on them. Add the rice to the onions and stir continuously for a further 4 minutes.

Pour on the boiling stock and bring the mixture back to the boil. Cover with an ovenproof lid or cover tightly with foil and bake in the oven for exactly 12 minutes.

Meanwhile, place the tomatoes in a baking dish and drizzle with 1 tablespoon of olive oil. Bake in the oven for 8 minutes and set aside.

Bring the wine and cream to the boil then stir in the salt. Scoop out the flesh from the eggplant and add to the cream. When simmering, add the rice and simmer until the cream has been absorbed.

To serve.

Divide the risotto between 4 warm serving bowls. Place a tomato on the side of each plate. Grate the feta on top of the risotto and top with fresh sliced oregano leaves. Drizzle with a little olive oil and serve.

Paella. p.104

Pumpkin and saffron risotto. p.102

Avocado risotto. p.103

Paella.

Roasted eggplant risotto with trellis tomatoes, goat's feta and oregano. p.105

Creamy mashed potato. Potatoes are passed over these days in favour of convenience foods that have a longer shelf life, such as dried pastas. But there is no substitute for mashed potatoes with the evening meal, especially when a tasty sauce needs mopping up. While everyone knows how to make mashed potato, there is another way to achieve the best possible result.

The trick to avoiding lumpy, watery, bland mashed potatoes does require a certain piece of equipment in your kitchen, but the extra purchase is well worth the money when you consider the result. A mouli is a French machine that forces potato through small holes to remove all the lumps. Though metal moulis can get quite expensive, I have seen a few cheap plastic versions in gourmet food stores that work well. Potato can be 'riced' in a short amount of time to retain its heat before being served.

If potatoes are undercooked, the result will be lumpy (even after being riced) as raw pieces will still be in the mash. When overcooked, potatoes start to absorb water, becoming waterlogged. Potatoes takes 15–20 minutes simmering to cook through, and a knife will pass through them easily when cooked. If you see cracks appearing on the surface of the potatoes, they may be overcooked. The best bet is to always use a timer. Set the timer for 15 minutes from the beginning of simmering, then check the potatoes. If they require more cooking, reset the timer for another 5 minutes. Stick to these rules and you should never have a problem.

Any potato will make a nice mash if the proper rules are followed. My personal favourite is the Otaki or golden potatoes. They are not always in season, but if you see them, buy them. They always make a fluffier mash, and you can't beat that golden colour!

I don't like to use herbs in mashed potato as I feel the smooth texture is so important in the enjoyment of the dish. The only option for me would be to use a herb-infused olive oil to flavour the mash as in the olive oil mash on p.112. Of course that doesn't mean you shouldn't experiment with herbs and make up your own mind!

Serve mashed potatoes with fish, pan-fried meats, stews, at barbecues or with any dish with a sauce.

Basic mashed potato recipe.

Serves 3–4

500g potatoes, peeled and quatered
pinch salt
35ml cream
35g butter
⅔ teaspoon salt
pinch white pepper

Prep.

Place potatoes in a large pot and cover with cold water. Add a pinch of salt and bring to the boil, then turn down the heat to a slow simmer. Cook potatoes until tender, about 15–20 minutes, then drain thoroughly.

Heat the cream and butter together in a pot until nearly boiling.

Mash potatoes by passing through a mouli or blend in a blender. Stir in the hot cream, butter, salt and pepper.

Mash can be made ahead of time and reheated when ready to serve. If the finished mash loses too much heat, put into a plastic bowl, cover with cling film and microwave until hot. It may need to be stirred once while heating for even heat distribution.

Substitutions.

Other root vegetables work the best in a combination with potato. The different flavours that come out when a potato base is used are really worth experimenting with to find your favourite mash or smash combinations.

Kumara

Boil equal quantities of peeled kumara and potatoes separately until cooked, then blend in a food processor together with the hot butter, cream and salt. Serve kumara mash with red meats, stews and braised meats.

Parsnip

Boil equal quantities of peeled parsnip and potatoes separately until cooked, then blend in a food processor together with the hot butter, cream and salt. Serve parsnip mash with any kind of fish, chicken or red meats.

Cauliflower

Boil equal quantities of cauliflower and potatoes separately until cooked, then blend in a food processor together with the hot butter, cream and salt. Use cauliflower mash to complement spicy and chillied meat dishes.

Pear

Poach 2 peeled and cored pears in sugar syrup for 15 minutes until soft then purée in a food processor. Stir into one quantity of the basic mash recipe while still hot. Serve with duck, pork or game.

6kg
equinox

Variations.

Olive oil mash

Substitute the butter and cream in the basic recipe with 60ml extra virgin olive oil for a creamy rich mash with a mild olive flavour. The oil doesn't need to be heated. Serve olive oil mash as you would regular mashed potato.

Horseradish

Add 2 tablespoons horseradish cream to the finished mashed potato recipe and serve immediately. Use horseradish mash to complement red meats, especially beef.

Roasted garlic

Heat the oven to 180°C. Peel a bulb of garlic, lightly toss in cooking oil and wrap in foil. Place garlic on the bars in the oven, then roast for 20 minutes. Don't rest garlic on a solid surface or the base will burn. When the garlic has cooled, blend in a food processor until smooth. Add the paste to the moulied potatoes before pouring in the cream and butter. For a plain garlic flavour, simmer the cloves with the potato then pass through the mouli together.

Innovations.

Cheese

Many kinds of cheese complement mashed potato. Either melt 60g cheese into the mash to flavour it or grate on top for visual effect and texture. Try tasty cheeses such as Parmesan, cow's feta, goat's feta, blue cheese or Cheddar. Use blue cheese mash with red meats, feta with chicken, and Parmesan and Cheddar with any meats.

Brown butter mash

Heat the butter separately from the cream and cook until the milk solids turn dark brown in colour. Do not burn it black or it will be bitter. Blend the potato in a blender then drizzle in the cream while the blender is still running. When the cream is incorporated, drizzle in the brown butter in the same manner. Season with the salt and white pepper. Serve brown butter mash as you would regular mashed potato – it has a delightful nutty flavour and an extra smooth texture.

Olive marble

Blend 20 stoned olives (black or green) in a food processor until smooth. Stir partially into the mash just before serving for a marbled effect. For an extra strong olive flavour, use an olive oil mash. Serve with red meats.

To experiment, here are some creative mashed potato ideas:

+ Kalamata olive marbled olive oil mash with grated goat's feta
+ Brown butter, parsnip and potato mash
+ Blue cheese, cauliflower and potato mash
+ Roasted garlic and Parmesan mash

Dauphine potatoes.

Serves 4

Dauphine potatoes are crispy fried potato batter balls that are delicious as the starchy part of a meal, hors-d'oeuvres or just as a tasty snack on their own. This classic French dish is a simple batter made of two parts: mashed potato and choux pastry. Choux pastry is an unsweetened batter also used for making chocolate éclairs and cream puffs so the end result is a light fluffy potato fritter that is big on flavour.

300g potatoes, peeled and quatered
pinch salt
1 egg
⅔ teaspoon salt
50g butter
150ml boiling water
60g plain flour
vegetable oil for deep frying
freshly grated Parmesan
freshly ground black pepper

Prep.

Place potatoes in a large pot and cover with cold water. Add a pinch of salt and bring to the boil, then turn down the heat to a slow simmer. Cook potatoes until tender, about 15–20 minutes, then drain thoroughly.

Mash potatoes by passing through a mouli or blend in a blender.

Mix the egg and salt into the mashed potato.

Place the butter and boiling water in the saucepan and stir over moderate heat until the butter has melted. Shake in the flour and whisk until a smooth paste forms. Stir the potato into the mix.

Heat the vegetable oil in a large saucepan. Using a dessertspoon, scoop half the spoon with mix, then using a second spoon push the batter off into the hot oil for a teardrop shape. Deep-fry for 3 minutes, turning once while cooking for even browning.

Remove potato balls from the hot oil and drain on paper towels. Keep warm in the oven while cooking the other batches.

To serve.

Place the balls on a plate, top with freshly grated Parmesan, sprinkle with black pepper and serve.

Smoked salmon with avocado salsa and mashed potato cakes.

Serves 4

Avocado salsa

2 avocados
1 tablespoon olive oil
1 tablespoon lemon juice
⅓ teaspoon salt
freshly ground black pepper
30g Spanish (red) onion
½ red chilli
1 small clove garlic
dill leaves

Prep.

Peel and deseed the avocados. Dice the flesh into very small cubes.

Place the avocados, olive oil, lemon juice, salt and pepper into a bowl.

Finely chop the onion, chilli and garlic and add to the bowl.

Roughly chop the dill and add to the avocado mix. Stir together lightly then refrigerate the mixture until ready to use.

Potato cakes

400g peeled potatoes
50g flour
1 egg
⅔ teaspoon salt
1 tablespoon cooking oil
200g smoked salmon
freshly ground black pepper
olive oil for drizzling
dill sprigs for garnish

Prep.

Cover the potatoes with cold water and cook on high for 15 minutes. When just cooked through, drain into a colander and run under cold water to cool.

Place potatoes into a blender with the flour, egg and salt and blend until smooth.

Heat a large flat-based frying pan, add oil and drop tablespoons of the potato mix into the pan. Turn the heat down to low, then after about 4 minutes carefully flip the cakes. A little more oil may be needed in the pan.

Drain the cakes on paper towels then transfer to 4 serving plates.

To serve.

Place the smoked salmon next to or on top of the potato cakes. Spoon the avocado salsa evenly between the 4 plates.

Finish with cracked black pepper and a drizzle of olive oil, and garnish with sprigs of dill.

Dauphine potatoes. p.112

Smoked salmon with avocado salsa and mashed potato cakes. p.113

Batters and fritters.

Fritters were originally deep-fried, as described by Cato in 200 BC. Roman scriblita was probably the earliest kind of fritter made in Europe, using lumps of moist sourdough bread which was spooned into hot fat and allowed to form random shapes. This sounds like a close relative of the doughnut and is probably where the recipe originated.

In medieval times, hot oil was used for cooking (when they weren't pouring it over each other in war). The first liquid yeast batter, using the whites of eggs, was made about the mid-15th century. The yeast batter was run down the cook's fingers so that five streams entered the hot oil, where they tangled and cooked. Sweet fritters were made with more eggs than used today and sprinkled with sugar, wine or ale and sometimes cream.

The French created a choux paste fritter base by the end of the 16th century. The same recipe used for cream puffs and chocolate éclairs has very little sugar content and works well as a savoury fritter recipe due to its light fluffy texture. By the18th century, choux paste was piped through a forcing bag.

The Japanese have also been deep-frying for a long time, using a high starch batter called tempura. This creates a splatter effect and a crunchy batter that doesn't colour when cooked correctly.

The name fritter derives from the Latin word *frigere*, which means simply to fry. Modern-day fritters take many forms from sweet doughnuts and fruit batter fritters dusted with sugar to savoury meat and vegetable-based fritters. It is also common to pan-fry fritters and finish them in the oven or under a grill. The ideal fritter should be crunchy on the outside while soft and spongy in texture on the inside.

Serve fritters with relishes, mayonnaise, mayonnaise-type dressings or salsa – any sauce with a little vinegary bite to it. Chunky salsas are also a great serving option with roughly cut salad vegetables such as tomato, cucumber and capsicum tossed in a little vinegar, sugar and salt.

Basic fritter batter recipe.

Serves 4

½ cup plain flour
1 teaspoon baking powder
1 teaspoon salt
1 cup milk
1 egg

Prep.

Sift the flour, baking powder and salt into a mixing bowl. Make a well in the centre of the flour and pour in the milk. Crack the egg onto the milk.

Using a whisk, gently whisk the edges of the flour into the milk and egg. This is the best way to avoid batter lumps. It takes about 5 minutes to gradually whisk in all the flour, moving from the inside to the outside of the bowl.

When everything is incorporated, the batter is ready to be flavoured then cooked.

...ing fritters

...e a medium-sized frying pan on the lowest heat possible and allow the pan to come to full temperature. The trick with fritters is to let them cook as slowly as possible. Because they thicken considerably during cooking due to the baking powder, fast cooking will result in raw batter inside the fritter.

Add about a tablespoon of cooking oil to the pan then swirl it around to cover the base. Use paper towels to wipe a little more oil onto the pan surface between batches, keeping it slick to prevent sticking.

Place large spoonfuls of the fritter mix into the pan and allow to sit for a couple of minutes. When golden brown on the bottom, flip over and leave for another few minutes.

If the fritters stick to the pan, add a little more flour to the batter. Remove the fritters from the pan and drain on a tray lined with paper towels.

Keep warm in the oven while cooking the other batches.

Substitutions.

Substitute the flour

Chickpeas

Use chickpeas instead of flour in the basic recipe for a fritter similar to a falafel. Purée 300g canned, drained chickpeas (or cook your own chickpeas) with the basic recipe ingredients. Add 1 tablespoon plain flour to help stabilise the mix, then fry using the basic recipe instructions.

Pulses

Cooked pulses such as kidney or other beans can be used in the same way as the chickpea method. Any dried bean is fine as long as it is cooked first. Always serve a wet sauce with bean and chickpea fritters as they are dryer in texture than fresh vegetable fritters.

Flours

Many different flours are available on the market today. Substitute the plain flour with rice flour, finely ground cornmeal or chickpea flour for non-gluten options. Or try semolina and buckwheat flours for a different texture and taste.

Variations.

Cheese in fritters

Cheese melts and sticks when it touches a hot pan. So only use grated Parmesan or pecorino in fritters for an extra flavour boost as they are hard cheeses and won't create enough moisture to affect cooking.

Green pea fritters.

Carrot fritters
Add 200g grated peeled carrot to the batter for an orange, slightly sweet fritter. Try mini carrot fritters as hors-d'oeuvres or an entrée. Serve with seafood, for example scallops, caviar or shrimps, topped with sour cream seasoned with lemon juice, chopped chives and salt.

Courgette fritters
Add 200g peeled and grated courgettes to the basic batter. Courgettes makes a plainer tasting fritter that works well as a vegetarian main course with tomato sauces or salsas.

Avocado fritters
2 ripe avocados
2 eggs
60g self-raising flour
½ teaspoon salt

Place the above ingredients into a blender and blend until smooth. Proceed as per basic recipe. Serve with seasoned crème fraîche.

Green pea fritters
Add 200g thawed frozen or fresh green peas to the basic recipe mix.

While peas can be blended and added to the batter as a mash, I like the texture whole peas give to fritters. Serve pea fritters with creamy or mayonnaise dressings or salsa. Very tasty with poached eggs for breakfast, and they make a good muffin substitute for Eggs Benedict.

Beer batter for fish
Whisk together ½ cup plain flour and 1 teaspoon salt with beer until it is thick enough to coat the back of a spoon. Coat fish in flour, dip into the batter and deep fry until golden.

Tempura-battered vegetables.

To make proper tempura vegetables and fish, a deep fryer is recommended, or at least a thermometer so the oil temperature can be controlled. The batter is made of equal quantities of flour and rice flour, but substitute rice flour with cornflour if not available.

The Japanese mix together the seasoned flours with iced water then whisk together minimally with chopsticks to form a batter that still may have a few lumps. The idea is not to over-whisk and stretch the gluten strands in the flours, and use immediately to maintain the crunchy effect. Use canola, soy bean or any inexpensive vegetable oil. Keep the oil at a low temperature of 160°C (deep frying with oil is usually at 170°C). The lower temperature allows the batter to crisp a little slower, and slows down colouring, giving the vegetables time to cook. Drain well, season with salt and eat immediately. Tough job!

To prepare the vegetables.
Whatever vegetables are used, wash and dry them, then slice very thinly. Pumpkin and carrot require more cooking than green vegetables so make sure they are sliced as thin as possible. Suitable vegetables are:

+ Chinese eggplant
+ Courgettes
+ Spring onions
+ Pumpkin
+ Red capsicum
+ Snow peas

Slice the eggplant and courgettes on an angle to make attractive ovals. Trim off the green leafy part of the spring onions and slice the white part to the tip to aid cooking.

Peel the pumpkin then shave quite fine.

Cut capsicum into 8 pieces, deseed and cut away any white pith.

I use snow peas as they are – the tip makes a useful handle.

Sweet and sour dipping sauce
¼ cup mirin (see p.185)
⅛ cup rice wine vinegar
1 teaspoon soy sauce

Stir the ingredients together until combined then pour into dipping sauce bowls. (continued on p.124)

Batter
¼ cup plain flour
¼ cup rice flour
1 level teaspoon salt
iced water

Prepare the batter when all the vegetables are ready for frying and the oil is heated. This allows the batter to still be cool when it hits the hot fat, causing a splatter effect.

Sift the flours and salt into a mixing bowl. Lightly whisk in enough water to make a batter thick enough to coat the back of a spoon. (The batter cooks slightly translucent, so it can't be too thick.)

Cook one vegetable piece first as a test. If the batter doesn't stick, it is too thin so add a little more flour. Dip the vegetables in the batter and fry one vegetable at a time. Be careful not to burn yourself!

Use a slotted spoon to scoop out the cooked pieces when the batter is crunchy, and drain on paper towels. Serve immediately with the dipping sauce.

Tempura-battered vegetables. p.121

Creamed corn fritters with trellis tomato sweet and sour salsa. p.124

Creamed corn fritters with trellis tomato sweet and sour salsa.

Serves 4

400g can creamed-style corn
½ cup standard flour
1½ teaspoons baking powder
½ teaspoon plain salt

Salsa
10 trellis salsa tomatoes
1 spring onion
1 chilli (deseeded)
2 tablespoons roughly chopped coriander
2 teaspoons white sugar
½ teaspoon salt
¼ cup white vinegar

Prep.

Mix together the creamed corn, flour, baking powder and salt to a smooth batter.

Use the instructions in the basic recipe technique (p.118) to cook the fritters.

To make the salsa
Cut each tomato into 6 wedges. Roughly chop the spring onion and chilli, add coriander then toss through the tomatoes.

Add sugar and salt seperately to the vinegar and dissolve. Toss the vegetables in the seasoned vinegar.

To serve.

Serve the tomato salsa on the side with the hot corn fritters – perfect for breakfast or a light lunch.

Trellis tomotoes.

Chilli sambal.

Spanish onions.

Trellis tomotoes.

Sweets.

05

Meringue pies.

Many 17th and 18th-century cookbooks contain recipes for lemon custard, but it was not until the middle of the 19th century that recipes for lemon meringue pie appeared. Most meringue pies are made with lemons. The tartness works well but other fruits also have enough acidity to flavour these pies – and look fantastic.

For sweet pies such as chocolate and caramel, I suggest using the mini pie option as they can be too rich if served in large portions. Mini pies are perfect as part of a dessert, as petit fours with coffee or as a sweet afternoon treat.

Meringue pies are made up of three components:

Pastry
I have used a sweet short pastry in the basic recipe. This is a flavourful pastry dough, quick to make and easy to roll out, and can be made in a food processor, electric mixer or by hand. Ensure the butter and water are cold and don't over-mix this dough or it will be tough after baking. A high ratio of fat to flour gives the pastry its crumbly texture and buttery flavour.

Filling
Usually tart and fruity. The meringue cooks in 3–5 minutes, which rules out any whipped cream-based fillings and most creamy dessert fillings as too much melting causes the pie to become soggy, and the meringue sinks into the filling which then overflows. The filling needs to be heat resistant and able to sit at room temperature for a while or stored in the refrigerator if not being eaten straight away.

Meringue
While you can use whipped egg whites and sugar to make a meringue, many tricks are needed to make a successful pie. The meringue needs to touch the crust so there is no shrinkage and the filling kept hot so the base of the meringue cooks. I have used an Italian meringue (sometimes called German meringue), which is partially cooked with hot sugar and far more stable to work with even though a little more work is involved. The end result is a more consistent, puffier meringue with much less shrinkage after cooking. Serve meringue pies with whipped cream or ice-cream.

Basic pastry recipe.

1 large pie serves 6

240g plain flour
120g cold butter
30g white sugar
½ teaspoon baking powder
30ml cold water

Prep.

Place the flour, butter, sugar and baking powder into a blender and blend until the consistency looks like fine breadcrumbs.

While the machine is still running, slowly pour in the water and allow the mixture to come together forming small balls.

Remove pastry from the blender and work into a ball of dough.

Tips for lining tins with pastry

+ Roll the pastry to an even thickness all over.
+ Cut away any broken or ripped pastry edges before transporting to the tin.
+ When the pastry is rolled, drape it over a rolling pin to transport to the tin.
+ Once the pastry is in the tin, carefully push it into all the corners so the pastry sits flat on the bottom.
+ When the base is pushed in, gently press your fingers over the pastry along the sides so that it sits snugly into the fluted sides of the tin.
+ When all the corners and sides are pushed in (for both individual and large pastry cases), roll a rolling pin over the top of the tin to get a smooth edge to the top of the tart.
+ Check once more with your fingers that the pastry sits firmly into the sides and base of the tin before chilling.
+ Keep pastry offcuts in case any holes need to be plugged during cooking.

The pastry needs to be refrigerated overnight, or for at least 2 hours, after it is pressed into the moulds. This results in almost zero shrinkage.

The process of making the pastry stretches the gluten in the flour. If the gluten does not get enough time to relax before it is cooked, the result is shrunken pastry. Sometimes shrinkage can happen so badly that the sides of the tarts disappear, leaving you with a pastry disk and nothing to fill!

Large pie

Makes 1

Roll out the dough and line a 20cm flan tin. Prick the base gently a few times with a fork to help release steam and reduce puffiness while cooking. If the tart tin is bigger than 20cm in diameter, you may need to increase the filling recipe by 50 per cent.

Individual pies

Makes 6

Roll out the dough evenly to 4–5mm thickness and cut 6 x 14cm rounds from the pastry. Press the circles into 6 x 12cm fluted tartlet tins. Prick each base gently a few times with a fork to help release steam and reduce puffiness while cooking.

Petit pies

Roll out the dough to a thickness of 4–5mm and cut circles with a 5cm circle cutter. Press the circles into petit fours tins, making sure they reach into the sides of the tins. Refrigerate overnight, or for at least 2 hours.

Baking the pastry

Heat the oven to 180°C.

The pastry shell is then blind baked, meaning it is lined with baking paper and filled with rice or beans to weight it down to avoid puffiness in the pastry.

Use rice for small pastries as the grains are small and can be pushed into the corners and use dried beans for larger tarts.

Cover the pastry including sides with 1 piece of paper so none of the rice or beans can escape. Pour the rice or beans into the centre and fill them to the top for small pastries or at least half way up for large pastries.

Bake for 15 minutes then remove the rice or beans and paper from the pastry.

Check for any holes in the pastry and plug with a little of the dough offcuts. Brush pastry with beaten egg and bake for another 5 minutes until the pastry is golden brown.

Basic meringue recipe.

Makes 24

170g caster sugar
30ml water
85g fresh egg whites

Prep.

Heat the oven to 180°C. Place sugar and water in a small pot and bring to the boil. Boil for 2 minutes.

Meanwhile, beat the egg whites with an electric beater until they form stiff peaks.

With the beater still beating, slowly pour in the sugar syrup. This partially cooks the whites so they only need to be finished quickly in the oven.

Keep beating until the mixture has cooled then pipe onto the filling as on p.134. Bake for 5 minutes.

Flavoured meringe

The best option for colouring meringue is food colouring. Use colours that match the dish or suit a certain occasion, for example pink for Valentine's Day, or yellow with Banoffi pie, p.133. For miniature chocolate meringue pies, I use red food colouring and rose water flavoured meringue as a gift for Mother's Day or Valentine's Day.

Here are a few options for flavoured meringue. Use very concentrated flavours, so only a minimum of water is added to the meringue to stop the meringue flopping:

+ **Rose water:** Whip ½ teaspoon rose water into the finished meringue.
+ **Essence:** Whip ⅛ teaspoon vanilla essence into the finished meringue.
+ **Citrus oils:** Good gourmet stores supply excellent citrus oils such as mandarin, orange and lemon. Whip ½ teaspoon chosen essence into the finished meringue.
+ **Vanilla bean:** Scrape the insides of 1 vanilla bean and whip into the finished meringue.

Almond custard meringue pie. p.136

Chocolate and rose meringue mini pies. p.132

Variations.

Lemon meringue pie filling
180g butter
10 egg yolks
2 whole eggs
180ml lemon juice
zest of **2** lemons
240g caster sugar
1 tablespoon cornflour

Place all ingredients into a medium-sized pot and stir continuously on a high heat until just below boiling point. The mixture should be very thick but don't allow it to boil as it will curdle. It may need to be whisked near the end, as the mixture will start to thicken very quickly.

Strain mixture through a fine sieve into a metal bowl, then pour into the tart cases and refrigerate for 2 hours before piping with meringue.

Chocolate meringue pie filling
120g dark chocolate
60ml heavy cream
¾ cup caster sugar
100g butter

Melt the chocolate and the cream together in a double boiler. Switch off the heat, leaving it to stay warm until required.

Cream the sugar and the butter until very pale – about 5 minutes on high speed with an electric beater.

Fold in the chocolate with a metal spoon until well combined.

Pour mixture into the pastry tart case or cases and refrigerate until set. Only half fill the tart cases with the chocolate as it will rise a little and can overflow when the meringue is cooked on top.

Innovations.

Berry meringue pie filling
3 cups berries (any berry is suitable except strawberries)
1½ cups water
6 tablespoons white sugar
grated zest and juice of **2** lemons
3 tablespoons cornflour

Place the berries, water, sugar, lemon zest and juice into a medium-sized pot and bring to a simmer. Simmer for 2 minutes then remove from the heat.

Dissolve the cornflour in 1 tablespoon water then stir continuously into the berries. Return the berries to the heat and stir until simmering again and the cornflour thickens the berry juice.

Simmer for 1 minute then remove from the heat and cool to room temperature.

When cool, fill the tart case or cases evenly with the berries, then pipe on meringue and bake.

Apricot meringue pie filling
400g dried apricots
1200ml water
½ cup sugar

Place all ingredients in a medium-sized pot and bring to the boil. Turn the heat down to as slow a simmer as possible, then cook for 40 minutes until all the liquid has evaporated and the apricots are soft.

Cool to room temperature then pulse in a blender until jammy in consistency. Blend until smooth or leave it a little chunky – it's up to you.

Spicy apple meringue pie filling
4 peeled and diced apples
500ml water
½ cup sugar
zest of **1** lemon
½ teaspoon ground cinnamon
¼ teaspoon ground cloves
1 tablespoon cornflour
2 extra tablespoons water

Place the apples into a medium-sized pot and cover with water. Add the sugar, lemon zest, cinnamon and cloves. Bring to the boil then turn down to a simmer and simmer for 10 minutes.

Mix the cornflour to a paste with the additional 2 tablespoons water.

Remove the apples from the heat and stir in the cornflour and water. Return pot to the element and bring to a simmer again. Simmer for 2 minutes, then remove from the heat and cool to room temperature.

When cool, fill the tart case or cases evenly with the spiced apple mix then pipe on meringue and bake.

Lime, grapefruit and orange meringue pie filling
Follow the lemon meringue recipe but replace lemon zest and juice with orange, lime or grapefruit zest and juice.

Banoffi and caramel meringue filling
180g caster sugar
180ml water
300ml heavy cream

Place the sugar and water in a large pot and bring to the boil, then turn down the heat. Allow to simmer until the sugar turns a dark caramel. Remove from the heat and pour in the cream – it will bubble and steam quite violently so stand clear.

When the bubbling has died down, return to the heat and stir until the liquid reaches the boil again. Simmer for 5 minutes, making sure all sugar has dissolved by stirring occasionally. Cool the caramel to room temperature.

When cool, stir the caramel again then pour evenly into the tart case or cases and refrigerate for 2 hours.

For a Banoffi meringue pie, top the caramel with sliced banana before piping on the meringue and baking. Without the banana, it is a caramel meringue pie.

Blackberry meringue pie. p.132

Coconut marshmallow pie. p.137

Almond custard meringue pie.

Serves 6

450ml heavy cream
1 teaspoon vanilla essence or
1 scraped vanilla bean
⅓ cup caster sugar
6 egg yolks
1 tablespoon cornflour
30g ground almonds
1 pastry tart or **6** individual tart cases from basic pastry instructions
30g sliced almonds for sprinkling
1 quantity meringue from basic recipe (p.130)
extra sliced almonds for sprinkling

Prep.

Place the cream, vanilla and sugar in a medium-sized pot and bring to a simmer then remove pot from the heat.

Whisk the yolks with the cornflour in a mixing bowl. Still whisking the yolks continuously, pour the cream onto the yolks. Place this mixture in a fresh pot and return to the heat.

Stir continuously over the heat until the mixture is just under simmering point. Don't let it simmer or it will curdle.

To check if the custard is cooked, tilt the bowl a little then put the pot flat on the bench and let the mixture on the side settle. Run your finger through the custard on the side of the pot. If the mixture holds the line of your finger, then it is cooked. If the line runs, it needs a little more cooking.

When the custard has finished cooking, pass it through a fine mesh sieve to remove any lumps. Stir in the ground almonds.

Pour the custard evenly into the prepared tart cases or case and let it cool to room temperature, then refrigerate for 2 hours. Sprinkle the sliced almonds onto the custard, and pipe on the basic meringue.

Sprinkle the meringue with the extra sliced almonds and bake for 5 minutes as per the basic recipe.

To serve.

Serve almond custard meringue pie hot from the oven, chilled or at room temperature with sweetened soft whipped cream.

Coconut marshmallow pie.

Serves 6

400ml coconut cream
1 cup desiccated coconut
zest and juice of **2** limes
4 tablespoons white sugar
2 tablespoons cornflour
2 tablespoons water
1 egg yolk
1 pastry tart or **6** individual tart cases from basic pastry instructions
1 quantity meringue from basic recipe (p.130)
extra desiccated coconut for sprinkling

Prep.

Place the coconut cream, coconut, lime zest and juice, and sugar in a medium-sized pot and bring to a simmer.

Stir the cornflour and water together in a cup. Remove the pot from the heat and stir in the cornflour and water. Return the pot to a low heat and stir until the mixture simmers. Simmer for 1 minute, stirring continuously, then remove from the heat.

Stir in the egg yolk then set aside for 5 minutes to cool.

Pour the coconut filling evenly between the tart cases or fill the large tart case. Refrigerate for 2 hours.

Pipe the basic meringue onto the coconut. Sprinkle the meringue with the extra desiccated coconut and bake for 5 minutes as per the basic recipe.

To serve.

Serve coconut marshmallow pie hot from the oven, chilled or at room temperature with sweetened soft whipped cream.

Jelly. Before instant powdered jelly became available, jelly was made by setting fruit juices with gelatine, so the colours and sweeteners were already in the liquid. While fruit is the most common flavour for jelly, there are many other options. Juices and simple sugars are used to create different flavours and colours, and an innovative twist is added by mixing fruit flavours with spices and liquors.

The basic jelly recipe.

Serves 4

If you do not have jelly moulds then there are a few other options using the equipment you already have. For individual jellies, set the jelly in small teacups, demi-sec espresso cups or small thin glasses. For a larger jelly, any glass, ceramic or plastic vessel will do, or set the jelly in a large mould and spoon out the servings as required.

Jelly can be very adult in flavours as well as perfect for the kids with a little imagination. Try setting edible flowers, berries and spices such as saffron thread, star anise or a cinnamon quill into the jelly for an elegant dinner party. Or, for the kids, sweets such as liquorice allsorts, wine gums and marshmallows can make jelly more fun. Everything floats to the top of unset jelly, so the jelly may have to be set in 2 layers with the apparently floating object on top of the first layer.

For colour-layered jellies, the different layers need to be made 2 hours apart and refrigerated in between so each layer has time to set. The jelly must be cooled to room temperature before being poured into the mould so the set layer underneath does not melt and the lines stay clean for a clever effect when served.

Serve jelly with ice-cream or whipped cream. Jellies also work well as a dessert with fresh berries and summer fruits dusted with icing sugar. For extra sweet jellies such as honey flavoured, serve with sweetened thick Greek yoghurt for a tart option that gives balance to the dish. Or, for a delicious low-fat dessert, serve with low-fat sweetened yoghurt.

Gelatine only lasts for 3 months after the bag is opened and can weaken even faster if the bag is not sealed properly. Always ensure the gelatine is fresh or it might not set the liquid in the basic recipe. If not used often, the best option is to purchase sachets.

Cognac and cherry jelly.

500ml water
½ cup caster or white sugar
2 teaspoons gelatine powder

Prep.

Place the water and sugar in a pot and bring to a simmer. Remove from the heat and stir until all of the sugar has dissolved. Sprinkle on the gelatine powder, then stir into the liquid until all the gelatine has dissolved.

Cool the jelly to room temperature then pour into moulds and chill. Cover the moulds tightly with cling film to prevent fridge odours affecting the flavour. If possible, allow the jelly to set overnight, or allow at least 6 hours refrigeration before serving.

To loosen the jelly, place the mould in boiling water so it sits as deep as the jelly is high and it releases from the sides, then slide it out onto a plate. Clean any extra melted liquid from the plate, or leave it and savour every last morsel.

Substitutions.

Substitute the sugar

There are always options for substituting basic ingredients in a recipe such as water and sugar. It is safe to substitute sugar with any simple sugars such as honey, golden syrup, treacle, maple syrup, jams or conserve jellies. If using jams, the finished jelly will need filtering with cheesecloth or a fine mesh sieve after making to remove any seeds or pith, leaving a clear jelly before chilling.

The bonus of using jams and conserve jellies is of course the colour. We are so used to seeing bright-coloured jellies made with artificial food colouring that I like to experiment with natural flavourings, which give the jelly colour without anything artificial added.

Substitute the sugar in the basic recipe for 1 cup liquid sugars such as maple syrup, jam or jelly. Substitute the sugar with 90g golden syrup, honey or treacle.

Substitute the water

Another option for colour is to substitute the water. Use any kind of wine for jelly by substituting the water with wine. Try white wine, red wine, cider, port wine, dessert wine or champagne in place of the water in the recipe. Or add the same amount of water to the wine and reduce to half to remove the alcohol content – I prefer to leave it in.

Stronger spirits and liqueurs can also be used to flavour jelly. Replace part of the water or wine with fruit liqueurs or flavoured vodkas in the basic technique. For spirits, omit 30ml water and replace with chosen spirit.

Variations.

Food colouring

The brightest colours come from food colouring, so use artificial colouring with, for example, vodka jellies. Add a couple of drops until the jelly reaches the brightness you desire. Particularly effective with multilayered jellies.

Fruit juice

Fruit jelly can also be made with fruit juices.

Juices such as orange, apple and cranberry can be used instead of the water in the basic recipe. All juice needs to be filtered, either through a fine mesh strainer or cheesecloth, to ensure the jelly is absolutely clear.

Fruit flesh
To extract the flavour from the fruit and into a clear jelly, simmer the fruit in the liquid.

To extract flavour and colour from fruit flesh, use double the liquid and simmer with 200g of the chosen fruit flesh and sugar until reduced by half, then strain.

For berries, only 2 minutes simmering with the basic recipe ingredients is required. This is enough time to extract the flavour and colour before straining. Stir in the gelatine before straining out the fruit to help remove any gelatine residue.

Fruit zest
Add an extra 200ml water to the basic recipe. Simmer fruit zests such as mandarin, orange, grapefruit or other citrus fruits along with the sugar and reduce the liquid to 500ml. Stir in the gelatine, strain and refrigerate as per the basic technique.

Innovations.

Spices
Sweet spices are ideal in jelly. Experiment with star anise, cinnamon, juniper berries, cloves, saffron or cardamom. Simmer the spices with the liquid to extract the flavour. As the jelly cools, the spice flavour will infuse into the liquid.

Keep the flavours of the jelly clean and simple by using 1 fruit flavour matched with 1 sweetener, 1 liqueur and 1 spice. In this way all the flavours have a chance to shine and will not cancel each other out.

Here are some examples to get you started:

+ Peach, white wine and honey jelly
+ Raspberry, red wine and treacle jelly
+ Fresh cherry and cranberry juice jelly
+ Apple and cider jelly

Add a little spice
+ Mandarin zest, white wine and star anise
+ Red plum, port and cardamom jelly
+ Dessert wine, saffron and vanilla bean jelly
+ Lemon zest, cider and cinnamon jelly

Champagne and rose jelly with nougat glacé. p.143

Vanilla bean.

Rose petals in ramekins.

Maple syrup, white wine and star anise jelly with caramelized figs. p.143

Champagne and rose jelly with nougat glacé.

Serves 4

Nougat glacé

3 egg whites
60g vanilla sugar (vanilla beans blended with white sugar then sieved)
60g runny honey
170ml heavy cream
30g ground almonds
60g blanched almonds, chopped
60g white chocolate, chopped

Prep.

Whip the egg whites with a beater until they form stiff peaks then, still beating, rain in the sugar. Keeping the beater running, slowly drizzle in the honey. Continue beating a further 3 minutes to make sure all the sugar is dissolved.

Whip the cream separately until softly whipped then fold into the egg white mixture with the ground almonds, chopped almonds and white chocolate until just incorporated.

Put the mixture into a freezer-proof container and freeze overnight.

Champagne rose jelly

500ml champagne or sparkling wine
90g runny honey
2 teaspoons gelatine powder
1 red rose
red food colouring

Use the basic jelly recipe method, but substitute the 3 ingredients with the first 3 ingredients above, then allow the jelly to cool to room temperature.

Place a red rose petal in 4 individual moulds and pour on one-third of the jelly evenly over the 4 moulds. Refrigerate the moulds for 40 minutes.

Add a few drops of red food colouring to the jelly left in the pot and set aside at room temperature until the refrigerated jelly sets.

Place another couple of petals onto the set jelly and pour half the remaining jelly on the set jelly evenly over the 4 moulds. Refrigerate for another 30–40 minutes.

Add a few more drops of food colouring to the last of the remaining jelly and set aside at room temperature.

Repeat the process with the remaining jelly moulds and rose petals, then leave to set overnight.

To serve.

Unmould the jellies and place on 4 serving plates. Place a scoop of nougat glacé on the plate next to the jellies and serve.

Maple syrup, white wine and star anise jelly with caramelized figs.

Makes 4

500mls white wine
1 large star anise
1 cup maple syrup
2 teaspoons gelatine powder
additional whole star anise for garnish
4 strawberry figs
caster sugar for sprinkling

Prep.

Simmer the first three ingredients together for 2 minutes, then switch off the heat.

Stir in the gelatine until it has dissolved, then leave the jelly to infuse the aniseed flavour for 20 minutes.

Place a perfect star anise in the base of 4 small ramekins. Pour in just enough jelly to cover the star anise and chill for 20 minutes. Make sure the anise is sitting directly in the middle.

When the jelly has set the anise in place, top up with the rest of the jelly and chill for at least 2 hours before serving.

Before unmoulding the jellies, slice each fig in half and sprinkle liberally with sugar.

Caramelize the sugar under a hot grill or with a kitchen blowtorch.

To serve.

Serve the jellies and figs with whipped cream or ice-cream.

Parfait.

The parfait technique is used here so the home cook can make an ice-cream without having to churn it in an ice-cream churning machine. This technique is based on egg yolks and is a very close cousin of ice-cream. Parfait uses whipped cream to aerate the yolks so churning is not necessary.

The earliest form of ice-cream can be traced back to the Roman Emperor Nero, and even earlier to China where snow was combined with fruit to make an early version of sorbet. A method using milk was developed, but ice-cream took its classic form in the English, French and Italian royal courts some time in the 1600s.

This form of ice-cream involved whisking sugar and egg yolks, then pouring on scalded milk and heating the mixture until just below boiling point. The yolks thickened the milk, cooking without enough heat to curdle the mixture. This is an Anglaise or basic English custard sauce. The Anglaise is then churned in an ice-cream machine so it freezes, but the ice particles are moved continuously thereby breaking up the ice crystals. The end result is a smooth, almost aerated, soft cream, until of course it melts again back to its original unchurned form.

Before ice-cream machines, the double bowl method was used to freeze ice-cream. One bowl had iced water and salt in it, the salt keeping the temperature of the water extra cold. The second bowl containing the cream mix sat in the iced salty water and was stirred and shaken for about 40 minutes until the contents were frozen.

In 1847 the first ice-cream hand-crank machine was invented by Nancy Johnson, and by 1851 ice-cream was being produced for the retail market. Ice-cream did not reach popularity until the 20th century when advances in refrigeration and power meant a dramatic increase in production.

Basic parfait recipe.

Serves 10

8 egg yolks
½ cup caster sugar
2 cups heavy cream

Prep.

Bring a large pot half filled with water to a simmer. Using a large metal bowl that sits inside the pot, whisk the egg yolks and sugar together lightly.

Whisk yolks over the pot of simmering water until the mixture triples in volume. It should be very thick and sticky after about 10 minutes of whisking, but not scrambled.

Remove bowl from the heat and allow to cool.

Whisk the cream in another bowl until just whipped.

Make sure the sabayon (yolks and sugar) has cooled, or the whipped cream will melt when added.

Fold in one-third of the cream so the mixture loosens, then fold in the remaining cream. Whisk until properly incorporated and the cream has thickened a little. Freeze overnight in an airtight freezer-proof container or ice-cream tray.

Variations.

The advantage of the parfait recipe is that you can melt ingredients such as chocolate and liquorice into the hot egg yolks to flavour the cream.

Vanilla bean parfait

For vanilla parfait, use vanilla sugar (vanilla beans blended with white sugar then sieved) instead of regular sugar in the basic recipe.

Bitter orange parfait

Add 2 teaspoons orange zest and 60ml Grand Marnier or Cointreau to the egg yolks and sugar in the basic ice-cream recipe before whisking over water. Proceed as per the basic recipe technique.

Chocolate parfait

After the yolks and sugar have finished cooking over the heat, add 200g chocolate and an additional 4 tablespoons heavy cream and stir over the heat until melted. Continue with the basic recipe.

Praline parfait

Praline is made by pouring hot caramel over the nuts of your choice, leaving it to cool, then blending to a powder. Add 90g praline powder to the basic parfait recipe when the cream is folded into the whites then freeze as usual. Works well as a combination with liqueurs such as Amaretto, Cointreau and Frangelico.

Innovations.

Cookie parfait

Add 120g blended chocolate chip cookies to the basic parfait recipe. Alternatively, use other flavoured biscuits, for example gingernuts, afghans or peanut brownies.

Meringue parfait

Add 120g crumbled meringues to the basic parfait recipe when folding in the cream, then proceed with the basic recipe technique.

Apricot and brandy parfait

Soak 120g sliced dried apricots in ¼ cup brandy overnight. Add apricots and brandy to the basic parfait recipe when folding in the cream, then freeze as per the basic recipe.

Cheesecake parfait

Substitute half the heavy cream with cream cheese. Beat the cream cheese for a couple of minutes with an electric beater on low until it softens, then slowly pour in the cream while still beating on low speed.

Whip the cream and cream cheese until thick enough to hold its shape when the beater passes through. Fold in the cooled sabayon (yolks and sugar) until just incorporated, then freeze as per the basic recipe.

Use your favourite cheesecake flavours for a cheesecake parfait.

Other flavours to try

+ 1 teaspoon mixed spice and 2 teaspoons cinnamon for Christmas parfait.
+ Fresh berries (avoid strawberries).
+ Use chocolate chips but make sure the sabayon has cooled before adding chocolate chips to avoid melting.
+ Ripple parfait with thick, well-reduced fruit syrups (see Poached Fruit, p.151)
+ Substitute the sugar with honey for honey-flavoured parfait.
+ Play with every kind of liqueur you can get your hands on. Add ¼ cup to flavour each recipe. Match liqueur to the appropriate fruit, for example Kirsch and cherry.

Some of my favourite combination flavours

+ Crushed raspberry and white chocolate parfait
+ Christmas spiced black cherry and brandy parfait
+ Bitter orange and dark chocolate chip parfait

Nougat parfait cake. p.149

Bain maree.

Dark chocolate and liquorice brownie with liquorice parfait. p.148

Dark chocolate parfait.

Dark chocolate and liquorice brownie with liquorice parfait.

Serves 10

Liquorice parfait
150g caster sugar
1 cup water
100g soft black liquorice
400ml heavy cream
¼ cup Black Sambuca
4 egg yolks

Prep.

Bring the sugar and water to the boil in a medium-sized pot. Add the liquorice and reduce the liquid down to half a cup.

Let the mix cool then pulse the liquorice in the blender. Leave a little chunky to add some texture to the parfait.

Lightly whip the cream with Sambuca to a softly whipped stage and set aside.

Separately whisk the egg yolks with an electric beater (about 7 minutes) until they are very pale in colour and tripled in volume.

With the beater still running, slowly pour in the liquorice and beat until combined.

Fold in the whipped cream gently until just incorporated so it remains aerated, then pour into a plastic container, cover and freeze overnight.

For the liquorice brownie
300g dark chocolate
100ml water
300g butter
5 eggs
1½ cups caster sugar
1½ cups plain flour
300g soft sweet liquorice, chopped

Preheat the oven to 150°C. Grease a 22cm square tin with butter then line with non-stick baking paper. Dust with flour.

Melt the chocolate in a bain marie with the water and butter then set aside to cool.

In a medium- to large-sized bowl whisk the eggs with the sugar on a high speed until all the sugar has dissolved (about 10 minutes).

With the mixer still running, slowly pour in the chocolate mixture and continue beating until incorporated. Switch off the beater and sift in the flour, then beat again until all the flour lumps are gone.

Fold in the chopped liquorice and pour into the prepared tin, making sure it is evenly distributed through the mix.

Bake for approximately 40 minutes – a skewer should come out with a little mixture still on it (similar to wet crumbs rather than wet batter) when cooked.

To serve.

Allow the brownie to cool before removing from the tin. Top squares of warm brownie with parfait and serve.

Nougat parfait cake.

Serves 10

8 egg yolks
½ cup honey
150g meringues
2 cups heavy cream
⅛ teaspoon vanilla essence
120g white chocolate, chopped
70g blanched almonds, chopped

Prep.

Line a 22cm cake tin with removable base with buttered non-stick baking paper.

Bring a large pot half filled with water to a simmer. Place a large metal bowl inside the pot and whisk the egg yolks and honey together lightly in the bowl.

Turn the water down to a slow simmer, keeping the bowl over the simmering water. Whisk until the mixture triples in volume and becomes very thick and pale in colour. It should be so thick it feels resistant to whisking after about 10 minutes.

Do not overcook the eggs as they can scramble. This starts to happen when lumps appear in the yolks.

Remove from over the water and set the yolks and honey aside to cool to room temperature.

Crumble the meringues with your fingers until they resemble rough breadcrumbs.

In another bowl whip the cream with the vanilla essence to a soft peak stage.

When the sabayon is cool, fold one-third of the whipped cream into the sabayon with a metal spoon. Add the rest of the cream along with the meringues, chocolate and almonds to the sabayon, then fold in until well incorporated.

Pour the mixture into the prepared tin and tap tin on the bench until the surface is smooth and the mix is evenly distributed in the tin.

Cover the top with cling film and freeze overnight.

To serve.

Gently heat the outside of the tin over a hot element, moving the tin in circles until the edges of the ice-cream start to glisten. Pull away the outside of the tin and pull the cake off the base by pulling off the paper. Slice portions with a hot dry knife, transfer to serving plates and serve immediately.

Serve with a long-stemmed strawberry in fresh strawberry syrup, or use any fresh fruit, fruit syrup or just plain whipped cream and sliced almonds.

Poached fruit and fruit syrups.

Originally, fruit was poached in sugar syrup to preserve it for the months when not in season. The basic principles of poaching fruit can be easily applied to fresh produce and an incredible range of flavourings to make a tasty quick dessert.

Poaching is a great way to deal with under-ripe fruit that is too hard or has not developed enough natural sugar to be eaten fresh. It is a technique that gently cooks foods in a flavourful liquid just below boiling point. Skin peelings can also be used to flavour fruity syrups for desserts through the poaching method.

Serve poached fruit as part of a dessert with whipped cream, ice-cream or custard. Poached fruit also works well as a condiment for cakes and tarts, or use chopped poached fruit as a base for fruit crumbles, trifles and fruit pies.

Time to experiment with your favourite fruit and flavours!

Here is a basic recipe for poaching using white sugar and water.

Basic poaching syrup.

One cup of poaching liquor will serve 4 people using 4 large pieces of fruit or 300–400g of smaller pieces of fruit. A poaching sugar syrup is generally 1 part sugar to 3 parts water.

1 cup water
⅓ cup white sugar

Prep.

Place the water and sugar in a large pot and bring to a simmer, stirring until the sugar has dissolved. Make sure it is at a rolling simmer before adding fruit as some fruits start to brown from lack of heat if added too soon.

In addition, timing is crucial if your syrup is not hot enough.

Keep the syrup just moving at a slow simmer once the fruit is added. Boiling the fruit too hard will cause it to disintegrate.

If you are not sure if the fruit is cooked soft enough, test by inserting a small knife into the flesh.

It is handy to keep a log of how long the poaching time of certain-sized fruit takes, so that when you next make the dish with similar-sized fruit you can set the timer and concentrate on something else.

Remove the fruit and reduce the fruit syrup until it is half the volume to use as a dessert sauce. Add the cooked fruit back into the syrup before serving.

Fruit and syrup can be served heated or chilled.

Substitutions.

Substitute the sugar with

+ Honey
+ Maple syrup
+ Molasses
+ Treacle
+ Soft brown sugar
+ Golden syrup
+ Jam (use a jam that only has one flavour)
+ Marmalade
+ Fruit jelly (preserves)

Substitute the water with

+ White wine
+ Red wine
+ Dessert wine
+ Cider
+ Mead
+ Port
+ Filtered fresh juice
+ Grape juice

Variations.

Apples and pears

For apples and pears which have been chopped into pieces or cut in half, poaching time is generally 12–15 minutes.

For whole peeled apples and pears, poach for 20 minutes then leave to cool in the syrup.

Stone fruit

For nectarines and peaches, less time is required as the fruit is softer, about 8 minutes.

Small seed fruit like apricots and mini plums, grapes or pineapple pieces only take about 4 minutes.

Berries

To extract the colour and flavour from berries, simmer 100g berries in the basic poaching syrup, then strain. Reduce the syrup to half then add the berries back into the syrup when cool. Serve either heated or chilled in the syrup.

Strawberries always cook differently from other berries due to their delicate structure. For poached strawberries simmer the not-so-nice berries for flavour and colour, then discard them and add the reserved better berries to the syrup before serving. Serve the fresh berries either heated or chilled in the syrup.

Fruit peels

The peelings of most fruits, for example peach, orange and apple (not melons or other hard-skinned fruit), can be used to flavour and colour a syrup and make a tasty sauce for a dessert. Simmer skins in the basic recipe poaching syrup until reduced by half, then strain for a simple dessert sauce.

Poaching combination fruits

Select combinations of fruit that complement each other and either poach together, or one after the other, so both fruits retain their colour. For example, poach orange slices quickly in the basic recipe sugar syrup for 2 minutes with cinnamon and sliced orange zest. Remove the oranges and reduce the sugar syrup down by half. Add 100g blackberries and simmer for 2 minutes then pour berries and syrup over oranges so the berry colour and orange colours are still intact.

Innovations.

Try these tasty additions to poaching liquors:

+ Glacé ginger
+ Vanilla bean
+ Grated zest of citrus fruits
+ Cinnamon quills
+ Whole cloves
+ Spirits
+ Liqueurs
+ Liquorice (don't mix with other flavours – just use water and sugar for pears and apples only)
+ Lemon juice
+ Saffron threads or powder
+ Fresh passionfruit

Be careful with combinations. Keep them simple as too many flavours hide the natural flavour of the fruit. Just select one option from each section as demonstrated below.

Some combinations you can try that work well together

+ White wine with honey and saffron
+ Red wine with brown sugar and cinnamon quills (for pears and apples)
+ Cider with apple jelly and cloves
+ Mead with golden syrup and glacé ginger
+ Dessert wine with white sugar and vanilla
+ Filtered orange juice with golden syrup, orange liqueur and orange zest

Saffron poached nectarines with rose meringue glacé.

Serves 4

Rose meringue glacé

3 egg whites
120g caster sugar
170ml heavy cream
1 teaspoon rose water
120g crumbled meringues

Prep.

Whip the egg whites to form stiff peaks then with the beater still running, rain in the sugar. Continue beating for a further 3 minutes to make sure all the sugar has dissolved.

In another bowl whip the cream until stiff then add to the egg whites with the rose water and crumbled meringues.

Fold the mixture together until it is just incorporated. Pour the mixture into a freezer-proof container and freeze overnight.

This recipe is at its best eaten within 2 days after making.

Nectarines in saffron syrup
4 nectarines
120ml runny honey
360ml water
1 pinch saffron

Prep.

Cut the nectarines in half by cutting around the stone across the width. Twist the 2 segments against each other, being careful not to bruise the flesh. One side should come off easily but the other side always puts up a bit of a fight. Use a small pairing knife to edge out the stone.

Place remaining ingredients in a pot, bring to the boil, then turn down to a simmer.

Place the nectarines cut-side down into the poaching liquor and simmer for 5 minutes. Turn the nectarines onto their round side and simmer for another 3 minutes.

Remove the nectarines from the poaching liquor and reduce liquor to half the volume.

To serve.

Reheat the nectarines gently in the syrup. Place 2 pieces of nectarine on 4 plates.

Pour the syrup over the top of the fruit and top with a large scoop of rose meringue glacé.

Port wine poached pears with Christmas spiced parfait.

Serves 4

Pears are available all year round, making this dish ideal for a northern or southern hemisphere Christmas. Serve the pears hot or cold with ice-cream. Serve the parfait cut into slices and set into a mould or scoop it into the serving bowls.

Christmas parfait
8 egg yolks
90ml brandy
½ cup sugar
1 teaspoon ground cinnamon
2 teaspoons mixed spice
2 cups heavy cream

Prep.

In a large metal bowl whisk together the yolks, brandy, sugar and spices until just incorporated. Place bowl over a pan of boiling water and whisk until the mixture triples in volume – it should make a very thick and sticky sabayon (yolk and sugar mixture).

Remove bowl from the heat and allow to cool. In another bowl whisk the cream until just whipped.

Make sure the sabayon has cooled before you add the whipped cream or the cream will melt.

Fold in one-third of the cream so that the mixture loosens, then fold in the remaining cream. Whisk together until well incorporated and the cream has thickened a little.

Freeze in an ice-cream tray or an airtight plastic container.

Stand the parfait at room temperature for 5 minutes before serving to make the parfait easy to scoop.

Port poached pears
4 pears
120ml runny honey
360ml port
1 cinnamon stick
zest and juice of **1** lemon

Peel the pears, cut in half and remove the core.

Bring remaining ingredients to the boil in a medium-sized pot then turn down to a simmer.

Place the pears cut-side down in the poaching liquid and simmer for 10 minutes. Turn the pears onto their round side and simmer for another 5 minutes.

Remove the pears from the poaching liquor and reduce the liquor down to half the volume.

To serve.

Serve the pears chilled or reheated in the port wine syrup with scoops of spiced ice-cream. I like to use a little of the spice in the recipe as a garnish, for example the cinnamon quill in this dish. Serve immediately.

Juniper poached plums.

Fresh figs.

Cherries.

Saffron poached nectarines with rose meringue glacé. p.152

Port wine poached pears with Christmas spiced parfait. p.89

Crème brûlée and custard pots.

A crème brûlée is a custard with sugar caramelized on the top, usually with a kitchen blowtorch. This dessert has become one of the most popular dishes in New Zealand restaurants. I call a brûlée without the caramelized sugar a custard pot as they are served individually in one-portion-sized ramekins (small ceramic pots). The correct-sized ramekins to use hold 150ml of fluid.

There are several basic methods of making custard, so I have narrowed them down to two of my favourite methods.

The most common technique for brûlée is the oven-baked method where egg yolks and sugar are gently whisked together, then heavy cream, scalded with split vanilla beans, is poured onto the yolks. The mixture is then strained, poured into ramekins and baked in a hot water bath until just set. The texture of the baked custard is similar to a milk jelly set with gelatine but with the added richness of the cream and yolks.

The second technique is not so common but it is my favourite. Egg yolks and sugar are whisked together lightly, and then the scalded vanilla cream is poured on. The mix in the bowl is whisked over simmering water until cooked, and then ladled into ramekins and chilled. Whisked custard has a rich thick texture like velvet.

Flavouring the basic custard is quite a simple matter, but in addition to the variations on p.160, stewed fruits, fresh chopped summer fruits, chocolate chips and berries can also be used for easy, fresh flavour options. The water bath method of cooking often means the berries or fruit can rise to the surface of the custard, spoiling the look of the brûlée. The whisked method makes it much easier to control this by keeping the filling firmly on the bottom of the ramekin.

Serve brûlée with poached or fresh fruits and biscotti.

Ramekins.

Tahitian vanilla and coconut brûlée with toffee pineapple. p.161

Chocolate custard. p.160

Caramel custard. p.160

Christmas spiced cranberry custard. p.161

Basic brûlée recipe.

Makes 4

500ml heavy cream
1 vanilla bean, split
6 egg yolks
100g caster sugar
1 tablespoon cornflour

Prep.

Place cream and vanilla bean into a medium-sized pot and bring to the boil, then set aside to cool a little and infuse the flavour of the vanilla. This is called scalding the cream.

Whisk the yolks, sugar and cornflour together lightly in a large bowl.

Rest the bowl with the yolks on a damp cloth then slowly whisk in the vanilla cream.

Strain through a fine strainer to remove the vanilla beans and any remaining yolk lumps.

Water bath cooking technique

Preheat the oven to 130°C. Pour the uncooked custard evenly between 4 ramekins.

Place the ramekins into a deep-sided baking tray. Pour hot water into the tray so it comes two-thirds of the way up the sides of the ramekins.

Cover whole tray with foil and bake for 30–45 minutes or until there is only a little wobble left in the centre of the custard. Once removed from the oven, take ramekins out of the water to cool. They will continue to cook and finish setting.

Allow to cool to room temperature before chilling. Refrigerate for 3 hours before serving.

Whisked cooking technique

Place a large pot filled to one-third with water on medium heat. Pour the uncooked custard into a stainless-steel bowl that fits snugly over the pot and set over the simmering water. Turn the heat down to just under a simmer (the ideal heat that won't cook the eggs too fast).

Gently whisk the custard as it slowly starts to heat. The purpose of the whisking is not to aerate the mixture but to stop the custard catching, plus to ensure even thickening. The custard becomes a little thicker on the bottom, then all of a sudden will thicken.

Whisk vigorously at this point then remove from the heat. Continue to whisk until the mixture cools a little as the heat of the bowl will keep cooking the custard. If the custard boils, it will curdle.

To check if the custard is cooked enough, tilt the bowl a little, let the mixture on the side settle then run your finger through it. If the mixture holds the line of your finger, it is cooked. If the line runs, it needs a little more cooking.

When the custard has finished cooking, pour into 4 ramekins, cool to room temperature and refrigerate for 3 hours.

To caramelize sugar on top of the custard

Coat the custard in a thin layer of caster sugar. For the best, even caramelizing results, use a kitchen blowtorch to gently melt the sugar without colouring it.

Sprinkle on another layer of sugar.

Once again, melt the sugar by rotating the blowtorch flame over the sugar.

When all the sugar has melted, caramelize it by rotating the blowtorch flame evenly over the custard until the sugar turns dark brown.

Variations.

Butterscotch custard

Place 240g white sugar and 90g butter in a medium-sized pot on a medium heat. Stir until the butter has melted and continue stirring until the sugar turns smooth in consistency and caramel brown in colour.

Pour in the scalded vanilla cream from the basic technique and stir until the cream simmers. Simmer for 2 minutes stirring until all the caramel has dissolved.

Set aside to cool for 2 minutes.

Pour the butterscotch cream on the yolks and cornflour (the sugar is already incorporated), then strain and continue to cook the custard as per the basic recipe.

Caramel custard

Follow the instructions for butterscotch custard but omit the butter and add ¼ cup water to the sugar instead. Simmer until the sugar and water turns caramel brown, then pour on the scalded vanilla cream from the basic technique. Simmer for 2 minutes, stirring until all the caramel has dissolved. Set aside to cool for 2 minutes.

Pour the caramel cream on the yolks and cornflour (the sugar is already incorporated), then strain and continue to cook the custard as per the basic recipe.

Chocolate custard

Baked custard: Remove hot cream from heat, whisk 180g chocolate into the hot cream then pour onto the yolks. Proceed as per the basic recipe.

Whisked custard: Whisk 180g dark chocolate into the finished cooked hot custard until smooth then pour into ramekins.

Orange and citrus custard

Add the zest of one citrus fruit of your choice at the same time as the vanilla bean. Proceed with the basic technique as usual.

Try mandarin for a twist in brûlée flavours. I also recommend quality citrus essence oils, available from specialty food stores. Add a few drops before the custard is cooked.

Passionfruit custard

Use the seeds and juice of 10 passionfruit for both techniques.

Baked custard: Add the fresh passionfruit to the cream before it is scalded. Continue with the basic technique. The seeds are removed when the custard is strained but the flavour remains in the custard.

Whisked custard: Place fresh passionfruit in the base of the ramekins, then pour the cooked custard over the top and chill.

Raspberry custard

Baked custard: After pouring the custard to be cooked into the ramekins, dot with fresh raspberries then bake as usual.

Whisked custard: Place raspberries in the base of the ramekins then pour the cooked custard over the top and chill.

Christmas spiced cranberry custard.

Serves 4

For the cranberries

1 cup craisins or dried sweetened cranberries
1 cup water
1 quantity basic brûlée recipe (p.159)
¼ teaspoon mixed spice
¼ teaspoon cinnamon

If sweetened cranberries are not available, add 30g caster sugar to regular dried cranberries. Bring the fruit and water to the boil in a medium-sized pot, then turn down to a simmer and cook until all of the water evaporates.

Watch the cranberries near the end as the water evaporates quickly. Stir to ensure they don't stick to the pot. The cranberries will now be swollen in size and a little mushy. Evenly distribute cranberries between 4 ramekins then refrigerate.

Follow the basic technique for brûlée but add ¼ teaspoon mixed spice and ¼ teaspoon ground cinnamon to the custard at the same time as the vanilla bean for a Christmas-flavoured custard.

To serve.

The cranberries will stay on the base of the ramekin with the baked custard or pour whisked custard over berries and chill.

Tahitian vanilla and coconut brûlée with toffee pineapple.

Serves 4

For the coconut custard

500ml coconut cream
1 vanilla bean, split
6 egg yolks
100g caster sugar
1 teaspoon cornflour

Place the coconut cream and vanilla bean in a medium-sized pot and scald the cream. Leave to cool for 2 minutes.

In a separate bowl whisk the egg yolks, sugar and cornflour until smooth. Rest the bowl containing the yolks on a damp cloth then whisk in the coconut cream. Pass through a fine sieve to remove the vanilla bean and any remaining yolk lumps. Use the whisking method to cook the custard then pour into 4 ramekins.

When the custards have cooled to room temperature, refrigerate until serving time.

Follow the technique on p.160 for caramelizing sugar on the custard for a brûlée effect just before serving.

Candied pineapple

½ golden pineapple
caster sugar for caramelizing

Cut the skin away from the pineapple then slice into 4 rounds across the width. Cut each round into quarters then coat the flat side with sugar.

When ready to serve, caramelize the sugar evenly with a kitchen blowtorch until it turns to a golden toffee. Make sure the pineapple wedges are not touching so the toffee doesn't stick the pieces together.

To serve.

Place each brûlée on a large plate, then pile 4 pieces of toffee pineapple next to each brûlée. Serve immediately.

Miniature candied orange pavlova puffs. p.164

The beauty of pavlova.

The most famous ballerina in the early 20th century was a Russian named Anna Pavlova. While physically not a beauty, it is said that when she danced it was not possible to take your eyes off her as her movements were absolute perfection. The airy, slightly marshmallow dessert was named after her.

Rumour has it that a Wellington hotel chef, inspired by the white tutu with green roses that Pavlova wore when she toured in 1926, created the dessert. It had a crisp shell, marshmallow soft centre and was smothered in whipped cream to represent the tutu. For the green roses, the enterprising chef used sliced kiwifruit (or Chinese gooseberries as they were then known).

Since then pavlova has become well known in New Zealand and Australia, with the addition of every kind of fruit to the whipped cream. The most popular fruit used are strawberries, fresh passionfruit and the traditional kiwifruit.

Flavouring the pavlova mix is not such an easy deal. The sugar cannot be exchanged with simple liquid sugars like honey as the recipe is upset by any water content. And don't think I haven't tried! Instead, add dry spices, nuts or fruit zest.

I am not a fan of chocolate pavlova. I don't think the cocoa powder adds anything desirable to the recipe and so I have not included it here.

Open your eyes to some new variations on this classic recipe, which is one of my very favourite desserts.

Basic pavlova recipe.

Serves 6

4 egg whites
120g caster sugar
extra 120g caster sugar
pinch cream of tartar
2 teaspoons white vinegar
2 teaspoons cornflour

Prep.

Preheat the oven to 150°C, ideally a convection or fan oven. Line a baking tray with non-stick baking paper and set aside.

Whip the egg whites until they start to form stiff peaks.

Using the first quantity of sugar, slowly rain in the sugar while beating the egg whites, and continue to beat until all the sugar granules have dissolved. This takes about 8–10 minutes.

Fold through the remaining ingredients gently until just combined.

1 large pavlova

Serves 6

Draw a circle 22cm in diameter with a ballpoint pen on a sheet of non-stick baking paper. Place in the centre of a baking tray.

Pour the meringue into the centre of the paper circle. Using a spatula or pallet knife, work the batter to the edges of the ring into an even flat disc.

Place in the centre of the oven and bake for 15 minutes. Turn the heat down to 120°C and bake a further 45 minutes. Turn off the oven and leave the pavlova in the oven to cool with the door ajar.

1 pavlova per person

Using a large cooking spoon, place spoonfuls of the pavlova mix onto a baking tray. There should be enough mix to make 10 individual pavlovas.

Place the tray in the oven at 150°C for 5 minutes then turn down the heat to 50°C and cook for another 15 minutes. Remove from the oven and leave to cool.

Pavlova puffs

Makes 20

Using a dessertspoon, drop large dollops of pavlova mix onto a baking tray.

Place the tray in the oven at 150°C for 5 minutes then turn down the heat to 50°C and cook for another 15 minutes. Remove from the oven and leave to cool.

Petit fours pavlova

Makes 20

For petit fours, drop teaspoon-sized spoonfuls of pavlova mix onto a baking tray (or if you know how to, quenelle the mix with 2 spoons).

Place the tray in the oven at 150°C for 5 minutes then turn down the heat to 50°C and cook for another 15 minutes. Remove from the oven and leave to cool.

These are perfect served half dipped in melted chocolate.

Variations.

Walnut and maple syrup pavlova

Add 90g chopped walnuts to the basic recipe when the cornflour, vinegar and remaining sugar is added. Proceed as per the basic pavlova recipe. Garnish the pavlova with softly whipped cream sweetened with maple syrup. Drizzle more syrup over the pavlova at serving time.

Lemon or lime pavlova

Grate the zest of 1 lemon or lime and add to the basic meringue recipe when the cornflour, vinegar and remaining white sugar is added. Proceed as per the basic pavlova recipe. Garnish the pavlova with sweetened whipped cream and lemon or lime curd.

Orange pavlova

Grate the zest of 1 orange and add to the basic meringue recipe when the cornflour, vinegar and remaining white sugar is added. Proceed as per the basic pavlova recipe. Garnish the pavlova with sweetened whipped cream and orange zest sugar syrup.

Innovations.

Brown sugar pavlova

Replace the white sugar in the recipe with soft brown sugar and whip the entire amount of sugar into the whites for 8–10 minutes. Proceed adding the cornflour and vinegar as normal for a more caramel-flavoured pavlova. Delicious with caramel sauce.

Saffron pavlova

Use the same technique as the basic pavlova but before commencing heat the vinegar until it steams, then add a large pinch of saffron and switch off the heat. Stir in the saffron and let it infuse into the vinegar for 15 minutes. Proceed as per the basic recipe.

Pavlova and mascarpone berry trifle. p.169

Saffron.

Cloves.

Dried cranberries.

Saffron frozen pavlova cream. p.169

Golden kiwi pavlova.

Pavlova and mascarpone berry trifle.

Serves 6

4 egg yolks
60g white sugar
200ml heavy cream
100g mascarpone
200g cooked pavlova (p.164)
250g frozen berries, thawed, or fresh berries

Prep.

Custard

Place the egg yolks and sugar into a mixing bowl. Using an electric beater, whisk until the yolks triple in volume, turn pale yellow and leave a thick ribbon when the beater is lifted from the bowl (about 5 minutes beating).

In a separate bowl, whip the cream until stiff then beat in the egg yolks and mascarpone. Continue to whisk with the beater on high until the cream thickens enough to hold its shape as the beater passes through it.

To assemble the trifle

Crumble the pavlova and cover the base of a decorative serving bowl with half of the crumbs. Pour over half the custard then place half of the berries on the custard.

Repeat the process with the other half of the ingredients and refrigerate until serving time.

This dish is best eaten on the day it is made to prevent the berries discolouring the cream.

Saffron frozen pavlova cream.

Serves 4

Here is a great recipe for using up leftover pavlova, or just an idea for something a little different.

3 egg whites
120g caster sugar
170ml heavy cream
120g crumbled saffron pavlova (p.165) (or any other flavoured pavlova)

Prep.

Whip the egg whites until they form stiff peaks, then with the beater still running rain in the sugar. Continue beating a further 3 minutes to make sure all the sugar has dissolved.

Whip the cream until stiff.

Fold the egg whites and crumbled pavlova into the cream with a large metal spoon until incorporated.

Put the mixture into a freezer-proof container or ice-cream tray and freeze overnight.

To serve.

Served topped with a dusting of saffron powder.

Plums.

Honeycomb.

Kiwi berries.

Hazelnut praline.

Cheesecake is an example of a recipe which has evolved in the quest for delicious food. Believed to have originated in ancient Greece, history recorded cheesecake being served to the athletes during the first Olympic Games in 776 BC. Centuries later, it is one of the most popular desserts in the world.

Cream cheese is not in fact proper cheese. Old-fashioned cream cheese was made by draining cream through muslin cloth and leaving it for several days until it became as firm as butter. Most modern cream cheeses are made from a mixture of cream, milk and sometimes rennet. Lactic acid-producing bacteria are then introduced to produce the desired degree of acidity. Although the bacteria is left to age, cream cheese is not a matured cheese.

Often cheesecake-making techniques are timely and difficult. The two main techniques are baked or gelatine-based chilled cheesecake. Many home cooks complain about gelatine lumps and overcooking, but cheesecake can be very simple as the basic recipe technique here shows. It has no gelatine, does not require baking, and is made up primarily of three ingredients in addition to the biscuit base, ensuring simplicity of flavour at its best.

Biscuit bases

There are so many different types of biscuits available today that I like to explore unusual-flavoured bases as much as unusual fillings for cheesecake. The most commonly used biscuits are digestive, but home cooks should not limit themselves to one type of cheesecake base.

For this book, I have had a great time experimenting with different cheesecake bases, some successful and others not so successful. I match the filling ingredients to the base, for example chocolate chip cookies with chocolate cheesecake.

If I use a spice in the filling, I use a complementary spiced biscuit in the base. I had great success with most types of biscuits that were not too plain in flavour. Many people use shortbread but when I tried it, it wasn't very tasty nor did it have a nice texture.

Chocolate-covered biscuits work as long as they don't have chewy centres. They make a softer-textured base that is easier to slice into portions. The downside is that the packets weigh less so more than one packet is needed to make up the weight in the basic recipe.

I suggest trying new flavours and experimenting with a variety of biscuits. Try peanut brownies, chocolate afghans, malt thins or any other plain or chocolate-coated biscuit you can find.

Basic biscuit base recipe.

Serves 10

90g butter
250g biscuits of choice

Prep.

Melt the butter on a low heat then cool to room temperature.

Combine butter and biscuits in a blender until very fine.

Press biscuit crumbs firmly and evenly into a round 23cm diameter tin with removable base. Smooth over with a spoon then refrigerate.

Basic cheesecake filling recipe.

Serves 10

400g cream cheese at room temperature
120g caster sugar
400ml heavy cream, chilled

Prep.

Beat the cream cheese in an electic beater on low for a couple of minutes until it softens and there are no lumps. While continuing to beat, slowly tip in the sugar.

When the sugar is incorporated, and still beating on low, slowly pour in the cream. The cream needs to be whipped until very thick as no gelatine is used in this recipe. Whip the cream cheese and cream until it holds its shape completely when the beater passes through the mix, and the mixture looks a little grainy.

Spoon mixture on top of the biscuit base and smooth over with a spatula.

Refrigerate for at least 4 hours (if possible overnight) before serving.

To release the cheesecake from the mould

Remove the tin by turning the cheesecake on its side over a hot element. This will loosen the cheesecake from the tin. You will see that it is loose when the edges start to glisten and the tin can be pulled away.

Remove the tin base by heating gently over a hot element until it loosens, then slide the cheesecake onto a serving plate. The sides may need to be smoothed over with a spatula before portioning.

Slice portions with a hot dry knife to serve.

Clean and reheat the knife in between each slice either by dipping in hot water or gently heating over a hot element.

Variations.

Chocolate cheesecake

240g dark or white chocolate
¼ cup water

Melt the chocolate in a bain-marie or microwave and stir until smooth.

Mix the water into the chocolate. At first it will seize and be tough to stir, but with continued stirring it will smooth out. This helps stop the chocolate setting too quickly when combining with the cold cream.

Take the bain-marie off the heat and set aside.

With an electric beater on low, beat the cream cheese for a couple of minutes until it softens then slowly beat in the sugar. Beat in the chocolate then slowly pour in the cream while still beating on low.

Continue as per the basic recipe.

Liqueurs in cheesecake

Add ¼ cup of your chosen liqueur at the same time as the heavy cream then continue with the basic recipe.

Pick flavours that complement each other, for example:

+ Orange liqueur with orange zest-flavoured cheesecake
+ Rum or kahlua with chocolate cheesecake
+ Butterscotch schnapps with caramel cheesecake

Citrus cheesecake

Cheesecake filling can be flavoured with the zest of citrus fruit, for example lemon, lime and orange. To flavour the basic recipe with citrus, grate and add the zest of 3 limes, 2 lemons or 1 orange.

In addition, I would usually add another flavour as I don't feel the citrus has enough flavouring on its own. For a lemon and lime cheesecake, add a spice like ground cloves or cinnamon to the mix.

Jelly and cheesecake

There are 2 options for jelly and cheesecakes. The first is to set a layer of jelly on the top of the cream filling in the traditional manner. The second is to ripple the jelly through the cream filling.

To set a jelly on the top of a cheesecake

250ml water
60g caster sugar
5 drops of food colouring (optional)
flavouring (rose water, liqueur, zest or fruit, see p.141)
1 teaspoon gelatine powder

In a medium-sized pot heat the water, sugar, food colouring and flavouring until it starts to steam, then remove from the heat. Sprinkle over the gelatine and stir until the sugar and the gelatine have dissolved. Pass through a fine sieve and set aside to cool to room temperature.

Using a spatula, smooth down the cheesecake so that it is absolutely flat while still in the tin, then clean the tin around the edges.

Pour the cooled jelly over the cheesecake and refrigerate for another 2 hours on a completely flat surface.

Chocolate truffle marble rum cheesecake. p.177

Honeycomb cheesecake. p.177

Innovations.

To ripple a flavoured jelly through the cream filling

Make a plain cheesecake using the basic recipe and leave in the refrigerator while preparing the jelly.

250ml water
90g raspberries or other flavouring
3 tablespoons white sugar
1 teaspoon gelatine

Make a jelly by simmering raspberries or other berries of your choice with the sugar in the water for 2 minutes. When cooled a little, purée in a blender until smooth.

Return the mixture to a clean pot on the stove. Stir in the gelatine until dissolved over low heat.

Pass the mixture through a fine sieve into a metal bowl and refrigerate until it is semi-set to the consistency of thick soup.

Pour the semi-set jelly over the cheesecake mixture. Using a fork fold the jelly into the cheesecake mix by working around the cake in circles.

When the jelly is partially worked into the entire cheesecake mix, tap tin on the bench until the surface flattens, then refrigerate for 2 hours until set.

Chocolate chip cheesecake

For a chocolate chip cheesecake, melt 120g dark chocolate in a bain-marie or microwave, then squiggle melted chocolate onto the surface of the cheesecake before chilling. Work the chocolate through the cheesecake, mixing in circles quickly with a fork. The chocolate will set while you are doing this, creating the chocolate chip.

Tap the tin on the bench so that the surface settles and flattens then refrigerate as per the basic recipe.

Combinations of flavours

Here a few creative ideas for combination-flavoured cheesecakes.

+ Gingernut biscuit base, saffron, orange zest, Cointreau and honey filling
+ White Chit Chats biscuit base, white chocolate cheesecake filling and rose jelly top
+ Peanut brownie biscuit base with Kahlua and chocolate chip filling
+ Arrowroot biscuit base with strawberry liqueur and strawberry jelly ripple filling

Chocolate truffle marble rum cheesecake.

Serves 10

Prepare a biscuit base in a 23cm diameter tin with chocolate chip cookies using the basic recipe.

200g dark chocolate
¼ cup dark rum
1 quantity basic cheesecake filling

Prep.

Melt the chocolate in a bain-marie.

Heat the rum in a saucepan until it just starts to simmer, then add to the chocolate and beat with a wooden spoon until smooth. Set aside to cool.

Prepare 1 quantity basic cheesecake filling (p.172).

Spoon ¾ of the cheesecake mix on top of the cookie base, then roughly smooth over with a spatula. Stir in the chocolate rum mix to the last quarter of cheesecake mix and beat quickly until smooth.

Pour on top of the white cheesecake mix and roughly flatten with a spatula.

With a fork, gently turn the mixture over a little so that the cheesecake takes on a marbled effect.

Flatten the cheesecake mix with a spatula then tap tin on the bench to remove any air bubbles and leave the cheesecake level and smooth. Refrigerate overnight.

To serve.

Slice with a hot dry knife to serve.

Honeycomb cheesecake.

Serves 10

Prepare a biscuit base in a 23cm diameter tin with chocolate malt thins (biscuits) using the basic recipe.

To make the honeycomb
90g caster sugar
1 tablespoon honey
1 tablespoon golden syrup
1 tablespoon water
½ teaspoon baking soda

Prep.

Line a metal tray with non-stick baking paper then set aside.

Put the sugar, honey, golden syrup and water into a pot. Place on a low heat and stir occasionally until the sugar has dissolved. Turn up the heat to medium and bring to the boil. Reduce the heat, then simmer until it starts to turn dark brown.

Take off the heat and add the baking soda.

Stir soda in quickly but, be careful, it will bubble ferociously as it is very hot!

Pour honeycomb onto baking paper and leave to cool to room temperature for about 30 minutes.

The honeycomb will need to be crumbled into small chunks before it is ready to use. To crumble the honeycomb, use your hands or a blender, but I suggest your hands as the honeycomb can dull the blades and the large lumps of crumbled honeycomb are the tastiest part of the cheesecake.

Prepare 1 quantity of basic filling (p.172).

Before whipping the cream until it is thick enough to hold its shape, add the crushed honeycomb and continue beating until the filling holds its shape firmly.

When the mix is ready, spoon on top of the malt biscuit base and smooth over with a spatula. Refrigerate overnight.

To serve.

Slice with a hot dry knife to serve.

Glossary.

06

Arborio rice:
an Italian high-starch, short-grain rice traditionally used for risotto.

Bain-marie:
double boiler where one pot sits inside another. The bottom pot holds water to steam the base of the top pot resulting in gentle heating.

Bocconcini:
fresh baby mozzarella balls.

Chorizo:
spicy Spanish sausage.

Concasse:
blanched, skinned, deseeded and chopped tomatoes.

Crème anglaise:
traditional English custard.

Crème fraîche:
French matured and thickened cream with a tangy, nutty flavour and velvety texture.

Florence fennel bulb:
specially farmed aromatic bulb eaten cooked or raw in salads with a subtle aniseed flavour.

Kecap manis:
sweet dark soy sauce.

Mouli:
French hand-held crank machine that forces cooked vegetables through small holes creating a vegetable purée.

Pappardelle:
pasta sliced into very thick ribbons, similar cut to fettucine but triple the ribbon width.

Pecorino:
Parmesan-style cheese made from ewe's milk instead of cow's milk

Prosciutto:
Italian method air-cured ham.

Roquette:
land cress.

Sabayon:
egg yolks, sugar and sometimes wine whisked together until thick.

Saffron:
an exotic spice made from the stigmas of the crocus flour. Saffron gives food a yellow colour and exotic flavour. Available powdered or as whole stamens, the instructions for use are the same for both.

Scald:
milk or cream heated to a simmer.

Sweat:
to cook vegetables in fat or oil over gentle heat so they become soft but not brown.

Shopping Guide.

07

Most ingredients mentioned in this book are readily available from supermarkets. Here is a selection of equipment and ingredients that may require a specialist store.

Arborio rice:
generally available from the supermarket, you can also find quality brands at delicatessens and specialist food importers.

Berries:
all recipes are suited to frozen and fresh berries alike unless otherwise stated. Only use strawberries in a recipe that calls for them, as they do not cook the same as other berries.

Bocconcini:
these fresh baby mozzarella balls are now available more readily in supermarkets. If not, they can be found at specialty cheese stores and delicatessens.

Chardonnay vinegar:
only a few specialist food importers and delicatessens supply a variety of top-quality vinegars.

Chicken stock:
ready-made stock can be purchased from the supermarket. Some brands need refrigeration and others don't. All recipes will work with ready-made stock as well as powdered stocks.

Citrus-infused olive oils:
available from specialist food importers.

Citrus oils:
available in concentrated form from specialist food importers.

Florence fennel bulb:
when in season Florence fennel bulb is available at most vegetable shops. Not to be confused with the wild variety that grows on the side of the road.

Fluted tart tins:
any good cookware shop will carry tart tins of all sizes. Also found in professional chef shops.

Grapeseed oil:
available from health-food stores.

Hazelnut oil:
usually stocked in good delicatessens.

Kecap manis:
sometimes available in the ethnic food section at Foodtown, otherwise try any good Asian market.

Kitchen blowtorch:
Enerco Gas sell blowtorches quite cheaply, and recently boutique gift shops have been stocking brûlée starter packs, including spoons and ramekins, as well as a mini blowtorches.

Mirin:
sweet Asian cooking sauce.

Mouli:
chef shops, professional suppliers that sell to the public such as Action Dimock, and cookware stores such as Living and Giving.

Pappardelle:
short pieces of broad ribbon pasta available from fresh pasta stores, some delicatessens and specialist food importers.

Petit fours tins:
petit fours tins look like muffin tins but are much smaller. They can be purchased from cookware shops, chef shops and are sometimes available from supermarkets.

Piping bag and nozzles:
chef supply and cookware stores.

Porcini mushrooms:
available from specialist food importers.

Prosciutto:
usually available at supermarkets. They will slice to order at the meat counter. Other stockers are delicatessens and specialist food importers.

Ramekins:
ramekins of all sizes are available at cookware shops and professional chef shops.

Rice wine vinegar:
sometimes available in the ethnic food section at Foodtown, otherwise try any good Asian market.

Rose water:
can be purchased from any health-food store.

Sherry vinegar:
available from delicatessens and specialist food importers.

Smoked paprika:
available from specialist food importers and at Foodtown.

Saffron:
available from delicatessens and specialist food importers.

Truffle oil:
available from delicatessens and specialist food importers.

Vanilla beans:
sometimes for sale in supermarkets, otherwise try delicatessens and specialist food importers.

Walnut oil:
usually stocked in good delicatessens and specialist food importers, also occasionally from supermarkets and from health-food stores.

Sabato:
importers of fine foods.
09 630 8751
sales@sabato.co.nz
www.sabato.co.nz

Action Dimock:
trade equipment available to the public.
0800 462284
www.butlergibpat.co.nz

Cucina Foods Ltd:
Fresh pasta suppliers.
0800 282462
09 815 0377
cucinafoods@xtra.co.nz

House of Knives:
chef suppliers.
24 Mt Eden Road, Auckland
09 302 2980
171 Jackson St, Petone, Wellington
04 939 3399
or Freephone
0508 564837
www.houseofknives.co.nz

Index.

08

A

Aïoli 34

Almond custard meringue pie 136

B

Balsamic brined pork chops with pickled baby beets and radish 89

Basic biscuit base recipe 172

Basic brûlée recipe 159

Butterscotch custard 160

Caramel custard 160

Chocolate custard 160

Orange and citrus custard 160

Passionfruit custard 160

Raspberry custard 160

To caramelize sugar on top of the custard 160

Water bath cooking technique 159

Whisked cooking technique 159

Christmas spiced cranberry custard 161

Tahitian vanilla and coconut brûlée with toffee pineapple 161

Basic cheesecake filling recipe 172

Chocolate cheesecake 173

Chocolate chip cheesecake 176

Citrus cheesecake 173

Combinations of flavours 176

Jelly and cheesecake 173

Liqueurs in cheesecake 173

To release the cheesecake 173

To ripple a flavoured jelly through the cheesecake 176

To set a jelly on top 173

Chocolate truffle marble rum cheesecake 177

Honeycomb cheesecake 177

Basic fish brine recipe 81
(See also pages 84–85)

Basic fritter batter recipe 118

Avocado fritters 120

Carrot fritters 120

Cheese in fritters 120

Chickpeas 120

Cooking fritters 118

Courgette fritters 120

Flours 120

Green pea fritters 120

Pulses 120

Substitute the flour 120

Creamed corn fritters with trellis tomato sweet and sour salsa 124

Tempura-battered vegetables 121

Basic hollandaise recipe 17

Basil hollandaise 18

Béarnaise sauce 18

Lime hollandaise 18

Works benedict 20

Wheaten blinis with smoked fish caviar and hollandaise 23

Basic jelly recipe 138

Add a little spice 141

Food colouring 140

Fruit flesh 141

Fruit juice 140

Fruit zest 141

Spices 141

Substitute the sugar 140

Substitute the water 140

Champagne and rose jelly with nougat glacé 143

Maple syrup, white wine and star anise jelly with caramelized figs 143

Basic mashed potato recipe 109

Brown butter mash 111

Cauliflower 109

Cheese 111

Horseradish 111

Kumara 109

Olive marble 111

Olive oil mash 111

Parsnip 109

Pear 109

Roasted garlic 111

Dauphine potatoes 112

Smoked salmon with avocado salsa and mashed potato cakes 113

Basic mayonnaise recipe 34
Aïoli 34
Avocado mayonnaise 36
Caesar mayonnaise 35
Changing mayonnaise into a flowing dressing 34
Chilli and lime mayonnaise 35
Citrus mayonnaise 34
Fruit in mayonnaise 36
Ginger aïoli 36
Herb mayonnaise 35
Lemon and coriander dressing 36
Pimento mayonnaise 36
Remoulade sauce 35
Spices in mayonnaise 36
Tartare sauce 35
Thousand island dressing 35
Green bean salad with gourmet potatoes, brown sugar glazed spanish onions, soft-boiled eggs and anchovy dressing 41
Prosciutto, bocconcini, bell peppers, black olives and baby spinach leaves with rosemary cream dressing 40
Basic meat (and fish) brine recipe 81
Apple juice 84
Brown sugar 84
Coconut cream 84
Garlic 85
Herb additions 85
Lemon juice 84
Maple syrup 84
Molasses and treacle 84
Orange juice 84
Root ginger 85
Soy sauce 84
Spices 85
Stock 84
Timing 81
Balsamic brined pork chops with pickled baby beets and radish 89
Roast turkey with prune and cashew stuffing with cider cranberry glaze 88
Basic meringue recipe 130
Apricot meringue pie filling 132
Banoffi and caramel meringue pie filling 133
Chocolate meringue pie filling 132
Flavoured meringue 130
Berry meringue pie filling 132
Lemon meringue pie filling 132
Lime, grapefruit and orange meringue pie filling 133
Spicy apple meringue pie filling 133
Almond custard meringue pie 136
Coconut marshmallow pie 137
Basic parfait recipe 145
Apricot and brandy 146
Bitter orange 145
Cheesecake 146
Chocolate 145
Cookie 146
Favourite combinations 146
Meringue 146
Other flavours 146
Praline 145
Vanilla bean 145
Dark chocolate and liquorice brownie with liquorice parfait 148
Nougat parfait cake 149
Basic pastry recipe (large pie serves) 129
Baking the pastry 130
Individual pies 130
Large pie 130
Petit pies 130
Tips 129
Basic pavlova recipe 164
Brown sugar pavlova 165
Large pavlova 164
Lemon or lime pavlova 165
One pavlova per person 164
Orange pavlova 165
Pavlova puffs 164
Petit fours pavlova 164
Saffron pavlova 165
Walnut and maple syrup pavlova 165

Pavlova and mascarpone berry trifle 169
Saffron frozen pavlova cream 169
Basic pesto and pistou recipes 54
Almonds 57
Brazil nuts 57
Cashew nuts 57
Chilli oil 57
Coriander 56
Dill 56
Flat leaf parsley 54
Hazelnuts 57
Lemon-infused olive oil 57
Macadamia nuts 57
Mint 54
Oregano 56
Pistachios 57
Roquette 56
Sesame oil 57
Skinned peanuts 57
Sunflower seeds 57
Walnut oil 57
Walnuts 57
Watercress 56
Salmon carpaccio with dill pistou, chilli, cucumber and lime salsa 61
White cheese pasta with roasted olives, capsicums and basil pistou 60
Basic pistou recipe 54
Basic poaching syrup 151
Apples and pears 151
Berries 151
Fruit peels 152
Poaching combination fruits 152
Some combinations 152
Stone fruit 151
Substitute the sugar 151
Substitute the water 151
Tasty additions 152
Saffron poached nectarines with rose meringue glacé 152
Port wine poached pears with christmas spiced parfait 153
Basic polenta cake recipe 94
Anchovy 95
Black pepper 95
Cheese 95
Dried mushrooms 96
Herbs 95
Mushroom 95
Pumpkin 96
Roast garlic 95
Smoked paprika 96
White wine 95
Roast pumpkin polenta cake salad with artichokes, caper berries, trellis tomatoes and sour cream dressing 97
Spinach and feta polenta with roasted black olives and sage butter 96
Basic risotto recipe 102
Avocado 103
Flat or button mushroom 103
Florence fennel bulb and lemon 103
Green pea 103
Lemon 102
Porcini mushroom 103
Pumpkin 102
Saffron (risotto Milanese) 102
Spinach 102
Watercress 103
Roasted eggplant risotto with trellis tomatoes, goat's feta and oregano 105
Paella 104
Basic smoking marinade recipe 68
Capsicums 69
Chillies 69
Eggplant 69
Garlic 69
Smoked freshwater fish 68
Smoked shellfish 69
Smoked white fish 69
Substitute the sugar 68
Substitute the sugar and soy sauce 68
Tomatoes 69
Smoked mussels in a chilli and garlic marinade 71
Smoked tomato ketchup 71

Basic stew recipe 73

Beef 74
Carbohydrates in stews 75
Chicken 74
Dumplings 75
Ham hocks 75
Lamb 74
Lamb shanks 74
Pork 74
Salted flavours 75
Vegetables 75
Coq au vin 76
Mediterranean pork stew 77
Basic vinaigrette recipe 43
Cheese 46
Curry powder 46
Egg yolks 46
Green herb 47
Japanese 47
Mustard 47
Sesame 47
Spices 46
Substitute the oil 45
Substitute the vinegar 45
Tomatoes 46
Rare seared eye fillet with mung bean salad and ginger sweet and sour vinaigrette 49
Smoked salmon and avocado salad with pecorino cheese, baby cos leaves and roasted tomato vinaigrette 48
Basic white wine cream sauce recipe 26
Avocado 27
Capers 27
Cheese 27
Combination sauces 28
Crème fraîche 28
Cucumber 28
Egg yolks 28
Fresh tomato 26
Herbs 27
Lemon 27
Liquors 26
Mushroom 28
Mustard 27
Pepper 26
Saffron 27
Sour cream 28
Vinegars 26
Smoked paprika seared chicken breast with pappardelle pasta, olives, rosemary and white wine cream sauce 29
Wild mushroom spaghetti with white wine cream sauce, parmesan and fresh thyme 29
Batters and fritters 116–117
Brining meats 80–81

C

Champagne and rose jelly with nougat glacé 143
Cheesecake 170–173
Chocolate truffle marble rum cheesecake 177
Christmas spiced cranberry custard 161
Coconut marshmallow pie 137
Coq au vin 76
Cream sauce 24–25
Creamed corn fritters with trellis tomato sweet and sour salsa 124
Creamy mashed potato 108
Creamy wet polenta 94
Crème brûlée and custard pots 156

D

Dark chocolate and liquorice brownie with liquorice parfait 148
Dauphine potatoes 112
Fettucine carbonara 28

G

Green bean salad with gourmet potatoes, brown sugar glazed spanish onions, soft-boiled eggs and anchovy dressing 41

H

Honeycomb cheesecake 177
Hot smoking fish and vegetables 64–65

J

Jelly 138

M

Makeshift smoker 68
Maple syrup, white wine and star anise jelly with caramelized figs 143
Mayonnaise 32–33
Mediterranean pork stew 77
Meringue pies 128

N

Nougat parfait cake 149

P

Paella 104
Parfait 144
Pavlova 163
Pavlova and mascarpone berry trifle 168
Pesto and pistou 52–54
Poached fruit and syrups 150
Polenta 92
Port wine poached pears with Christmas spiced parfait 153
Prosciutto, bocconcini, red capsicums, black olives and baby spinach leaves with rosemary cream dressing 40

R

Rare seared eye fillet with mung bean salad and ginger sweet and sour vinaigrette 49
Risotto 100–103
Roast pumpkin polenta cake salad with artichokes, caper berries, trellis tomatoes and sour cream dressing 97
Roast turkey with prune and cashew stuffing with cider cranberry glaze 88
Roasted eggplant risotto with trellis tomatoes, goat's feta and oregano 105

S

Saffron frozen pavlova cream 169
Saffron poached nectarines with rose meringue glacé 152
Salmon carpaccio with dill pistou, chilli, cucumber and lime salsa 61
Slow-cooked meats 72–73
Smoked mussels in a chilli and garlic marinade 71
Smoked paprika seared chicken breast with pappardelle pasta, olives, rosemary and white wine cream sauce 29
Smoked salmon and avocado salad with pecorino cheese, baby cos leaves and roasted tomato vinaigrette 48
Smoked salmon with avocado salsa and mashed potato cakes 113
Smoked tomato ketchup 71
Spinach and feta polenta with roasted black olives and sage butter 96

T

Tahitian vanilla and coconut brûlée with toffee pineapple 161
Tempura-battered vegetables 121
Tomato concasse 26

V

Vinaigrette 42–43

W

Wheaten blinis with smoked tuna caviar and hollandaise 23
White cheese pasta with roasted olives, capsicums and basil pistou 60
Wild mushroom spaghetti with white wine cream sauce, parmesan and fresh thyme 29
Works benedict 20